the computer book

an introduction to computers and computing

Robin Bradbeer
Peter De Bono
Peter Laurie

Additional material and editing by
Susan Curran
David Allen BBC

British Broadcasting Corporation

I should like to thank Fiona, Bob, Chris, Geoff, John, Matt, Mel, Paul, Richard and other colleagues and friends who have helped in the preparation and checking of the material for this book, and in particular Desmond Green (for photographic research) and the designer, Roger Fletcher, assisted by Nigel Swift.

David Allen

This book is published in conjunction with the BBC television series *The Computer Programme* first transmitted on BBC-2 from January 1982 and produced by Paul Kriwaczek

Editor of the *BBC Computer Literacy Project*: David Allen

Published to accompany a series of programmes prepared in consultation with the BBC Continuing Education Advisory Council

First published 1982. Reprinted 1982
Published by the British Broadcasting Corporation
35 Marylebone High Street, London W1M 4AA

Filmset by August Filmsetting, Warrington, Cheshire
in 11/12pt Apollo Monophoto
Printed in Scotland by Thomson Litho Limited, East Kilbride
ISBN 0 563 16484 0

Contents

Introduction

Microelectronics, the silicon chip technology which has made the cheap microcomputer possible, is transforming the economy of the industrialised nations and increasingly affecting the jobs and the lives of many people. Computing power is virtually the only commodity which is falling in cost each year. It's now becoming so cheap that the personal microcomputer is something that will soon find its way into innumerable homes. Even now it's in high street shops rubbing shoulders with its slightly younger brothers, the calculators and the digital watches, which were virtually unknown a decade ago. Unlike them, it offers a growing number of people an intellectual challenge as well as being a practical and versatile new tool just as capable of controlling *things* as of juggling with information.

In terms of computing power what the big computer does today the little computer could do tomorrow. Whether big or small, all computers function in very similar ways. But what can they do? How do they work? How can they be used in solving problems? Where is the technology taking us? What are its limitations? The purpose of this book (and the television series it accompanies) is to answer these questions and to encourage a new kind of literacy – 'computer literacy'.

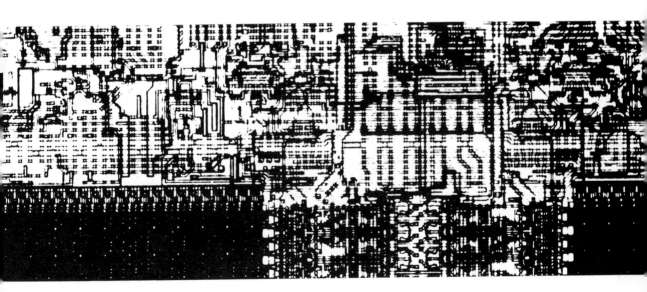

Why 'computer literacy'?

Since microcomputers and other similar devices are not very different from many other technological innovations that have changed the face of society, it helps to look back in history. The last time something as dramatic as this happened was perhaps when engineering got into business during the Industrial Revolution. At that time a small group of predominantly youthful men who mastered a new technology were vigorously transforming their world. Consider Brunel who, at the age of 27, was the chief engineer of the Great Western Railway, hurling his broad gauge lines like spears across a landscape that had not changed since the time of the enclosures. What did their contemporaries think of these arrogant youngsters, with their new ideas and amazing powers?

Ordinary, well-educated people then lacked the 'engineering literacy' which we all have now. They thought that to travel faster than 30 mph would kill you. They thought the pressure of

The heirs to the Industrial Revolution.
Shareholders riding in a broad gauge train try out the Metropolitan Line, London's first underground railway, just before the opening on January 10th, 1863

steam in a boiler would infallibly burst it. They 'knew' that steel ships would sink. On the other hand, they thought it not unlikely that a man could pedal hard enough to lift himself into the air.

Their notions were shapeless because they did not understand the basic laws of physics – simple enough laws that most of us now absorb from our culture without even knowing that we have done so. Do you not, for instance, at least have a vague idea how an old-fashioned clock works? Even if you are not a mechanic you have some notion of cog wheels driving each other: a spring, a pendulum swinging to and fro, and so on. Few people nowadays are baffled by a steam locomotive or a petrol engine, even if they do not know the subtleties of its operation.

We are the heirs to nearly 200 years of engineering literacy; we can distinguish the practical from the absurd; we have a grasp of the basic rules and can apply them sensibly to situations we see around us. Computing is just the same, except that only a few of us have yet been let into the basic secrets. The result is

The heirs to the Microelectronics Revolution.
Learning to use the computer in the primary school.

exactly the same attitudes that could be found at the start of engineering: belief in the impossible, refusal to believe the obvious – a general instability of opinion. However, it all turned out to be quite easy last time; computing need be no different.

What we are trying to do in this book is to show that the fundamentals are not as difficult as many people might think. Of course, we can't, in this short introduction, teach you to build your own computer; but that is something few of us need to know, just as most people manage to drive a car perfectly well without knowing how to build one – or even, in most cases, how to repair it.

We hope to put across some of the basic ideas which will enable you to treat the computer as a tool which you will come across more and more often, and which you will find useful in your daily life – much, in fact, as we treat cars today.

Some readers will doubtless have access to computers – either their own computers, or computers at their school, college or work. We hope this book will give them some interesting new ideas. However, it is not necessary to make use of a computer to follow the book, nor do we assume that you already know anything about computers, about electronics, or about mathematics.

This is not a practical handbook to any particular computer. It is not a course in computer programming (though we do look at the basics of programming). It is an introduction to computers, what they are and what they do, which we hope will give you the confidence to go on and learn more. If you choose not to learn more, what you read here should still give you an insight into the new technology which is fast changing our modern world.

Using this book

This book is not intended just for you to read through from cover to cover. Of course, you can read it through chapter by chapter, and it will make sense if you do. We hope you will use it, too, as a source of reference, to dip into when you need some explanation. With this in mind, we have tried to provide plenty of cross-references.

The glossary at the back should provide an explanation of many of the technical words used in computing. In the text we try to keep these to a minimum and to explain them as they first occur.

1 Setting the scene

Computers are essentially stupid. They only do what they are told to do in instructions given to them by human beings. Nevertheless, the things they *can* do – and are being asked to do today – are many and various and are vital to our modern way of life.

Working out the weather

On the evening's television weather spot we see the pictures from space of clouds and winds and then the presenters' maps with their symbols for sleet, hurricane, rain and fog. Although the computer doesn't come forward to take its bow, it has done most of the work that leads up to the predictions.

The process starts with the collection of weather information. Hundreds of weather stations round the world – on light ships, at airports, in military posts – send information to their national weather centres by radio and telex. Satellites take pictures of cloud patterns and, using infra-red cameras, of the temperature of the earth below. This information is stored in the satellite by a small computer and transmitted by radio to earth-based stations when the satellite is overhead. Staff at these stations forward it by radio and telex to the weather centre.

In the weather centre, a picture of today's weather is built up in the computer – a very big computer this time, for the problem is enormous. Values for the air pressure, temperature, wind speed and direction and humidity for the hundreds of weather stations are fed in. The computer fits them all into a big overall pattern. It then has to do a most complicated calculation: taking the current conditions in the air over each kilometre square of the earth's surface it has to calculate – using the well-known laws of physics – what effect the air masses in neighbouring squares will have on it, and vice versa. This involves such calculation and recalculation that it needs to be done on the very largest machines if the calculation is to be done faster than the weather happens outside the computer room. Even then, the forecast is not terribly accurate, but it's better than wetting a finger and holding it up to the wind. At the end of all this, the

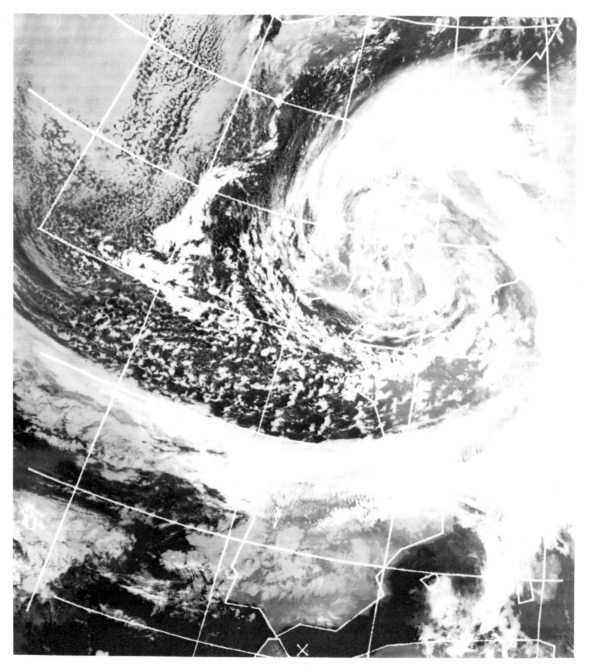

Deep depression over Britain – as seen by a weather satellite.

weather forecaster can say 'Light winds, some showers and bright spells – warmer than yesterday'.

Keeping the engine cool

In films, the dashing pilot puts on his dark glasses, vaults into the cockpit of his aircraft and zooms off into the blue. In real life he has a few more things to do. One of them is managing his jet engines, for they are temperamental beasts. As the aircraft accelerates down the runway, air is blown into the engine intakes at greater pressure and in larger volume because the aircraft is moving forwards. At the same time, the jet flow comes out more easily and therefore the machine gives more thrust. This means that the internal temperature changes. If the fuel inside the engine burns too hot the turbines melt; if it burns too cold the engine doesn't give enough thrust. So, as well as guiding the aircraft down the runway, the pilot has to juggle with the fuel flow to keep the turbine temperature just right.

Life is made much easier and safer for the dashing aeronaut – and for his passengers – if a computer takes over the whole job. It will have temperature sensors in the combustion chamber. It will measure the temperature and pressure of the outside air (a jet engine gives much less thrust at a hot, high airport like Khartoum in the Sudan than a cold, low one like Benbecula in the Hebrides). It will measure the forward push of the engine by measuring the pressure in the final jet tube. It will measure the fuel flow and the air speed, and the weight of the aircraft. With all these figures, the computer will calculate and deliver the right amount of fuel to the engine each second. Meanwhile, the pilot can concentrate on getting the passengers from A to B without alarm or dismemberment.

Computers take to the air. Concorde has 8 on-board computers to help with navigation, communications and the control of cabin conditions like pressure, as well as control of the engines.

Right – the man-powered Gossamer Condor was designed with the aid of a computer. Above – three dimensional representations of the plane from the computer's screen.

Tracking the traffic

Once in the air, our hawk-eyed friend rushes along at 600 mph. His brother bird-men, rushing at 600 mph – possibly in the opposite direction – have little chance of seeing him coming. If fate wills that their paths cross, an accident is almost inevitable.

To prevent these mishaps, nations with brisk air-transport businesses provide an air traffic control service. This consists of a network of radars whose plots are brought to one or two central offices, where people well trained in mental gymnastics keep track of each aircraft and steer it round those other – invisible – aircraft that might bang into it. Usually they are successful; very occasionally they fail.

In recent years, experiments have been made with *automatic* air traffic control – at least with the collision avoidance part. A

The latest generation of air-traffic control radar equipment being tested. Aircraft do not just appear as 'blips' on the screen; their flight numbers and heights appear as well, as a result of signals coming from the planes themselves.

computer watches the radars, calculates the position of each aircraft, 5, 10, 15 minutes ahead and warns the controller if a collision (or a 'conflict' as it is known technically) is likely. The controller can then try out various decisions – if he orders aircraft A to turn 10 degrees to port and climb 500 feet to avoid B, will it now collide with aircraft K?

The computing required to do this isn't easy. For a start, the blips on the screens as the radars go round and round have to be joined up with each other. They may deflect from the straight lines that you'd expect. The blip may disappear altogether from time to time; the computer has to be able to work out where the aircraft may have gone in the meantime so that when the blips reappear they can be attached to the right track. When two tracks cross, the computer must not think that two aircraft flew up to each other and turned round. On the other hand, if that's what happened, the computer must be able to follow it! It's no good the controller telling BA323 to turn left, when the blip he's looking at is actually KL96. This kind of predictive computing requires a powerful machine and well written programs.

The search for Mr Right

Computers are best at doing massive, highly defined jobs. One of the best examples is searching through a telephone directory to find a number. Of course, the computer needs to have all its information stored in its electronic memory and not on paper, but once the information is there it can search very fast indeed. It can even be asked to find a number when the exact spelling of the name is not known. Take Mr Bryzinski – or is it Brznski? Type in the name as accurately as you know it and a reasonably modest modern computer with the right program will find the number in a few seconds or will list out the alternatives. If you know an initial or part of his address it will then give you just the man you're looking for, his number and his address.

Can you imagine a more redundant and costly source of useless information than the London telephone directory – nearly 4,000 pages of telephone numbers, many out of date and only a few of which you will ever look up? Not surprisingly, therefore, the French Post Office has proposed to issue every telephone owner with an electronic way of finding telephone numbers using a keyboard and a small screen attached to the telephone which can communicate with a central computer. They claim the costs will easily be borne by the savings in paper by not printing directories. Electronic directory enquiries enable other, usually impossibly tedious searches to be made. Knowing just an address could enable the user to find the name and number of the owner of a house just as easily. Equally, a search for all the Dukes in London, involving looking at every entry, would take about half a minute. These last two searches would normally not be carried out for you for ethical as well as practical reasons by the human directory enquiries service. Yet the information is there, publicly, in the telephone book. Looking for it using hand and eye might be a week's work; for the computer it's no bother at all.

Home 'phone of the future?
One prototype for the proposed all-in-one French telephone system. Besides the electronic directory enquiries service, subscribers will be able to send typed messages electronically and receive pages of information on the screen – rather like that on Prestel.

Bars on the beercans

Have you noticed how soup and cornflake packets have started decorating themselves with smart patterns of black lines? They haven't joined some secret army – it's a way of identifying the goods using bar codes, in a way the computer can read with relative ease. How does it read the bar code? A simple optical wand, which looks like a fat biro attached to the computer by a wire, has inside it a light and a lens to focus the image of the bars on to an electronic sensor. As the shop assistant runs the tip of the wand across the bars, the sensing element detects the alternation of dark and light. The differing widths of the bars form the code of a number (which is often also printed at one

Bar codes on the groceries being 'read' by passing them over a laser beam – which is faster and easier to use than a wand. The beam is reflected back to a photo sensor. The result for the customer is faster service and an itemised till slip – useful for next week's shopping list.

side of the pattern). That number identifies the particular item to the machine.

What's the point of all this? Well, it means that the owner of the shop can change his prices whenever he likes. Instead of having to employ people to go round – at great expense – to stick new labels on old tins of soup, he just tells the computer that the produce with the bar code '34217854' now costs 19p instead of 17p. When the check-out girl reads that code into the machine

with a wipe of the wand, 19p will appear on the till and the customer's slip will have a full, printed description of what's been bought.

The same effect could have been produced by asking the girl to type '34217854' – but experience shows that she'll just as likely type '34271854', which might be the code for nylon stockings at £1.12.

Bar codes also make it possible for the shop operator to keep instant accurate records of what he has on his shelves. He can see instantly which lines are selling, and which are not. He need keep in stock only what he needs; in these days of high interest rates, shops make money more by cutting down their stock holding than by increasing their sales.

POS BUSINESS TEAM

    BAKERY   .29½
    HOME N WEAR   1.95 *
    PROCESS PEAS   .15
    GARDEN PEAS   .15½
    MIXED VEG.   .15
    M/ROOM SOUP   .23
    MEAT   2.00
    RICE KRISPIS   .65½
    GARDEN PEAS   .15½
    BABY FOOD   .16

    TOTAL   5.90

    CASH   6.00 T
    CHANGE DUE   .10

11/09/81 11:24 0001 1   3458   12
FUNCTIONAL TEST

SBURY BROADFIELD

DAZ AUTO E 3   .55
COMFORT 1LTR
CK/POT S/NOF   .41
OMFORT 1LTR   .27
RUIT & VEG   .41
RANULTD SGR   .06
UNKY   .40
                 .21
                2.31

ID   2.31
                 .00
25 0009/19
ALL AGAIN*

One idea for the future – a bar-coded Radio Times.
A few wipes of the wand feed the computer in the special radio receiver with the menu of programmes not to be missed during the week. It then knows when to switch on and off. Note that the first part of each code is the same – it identifies the frequency. Right – how the light from the wand is reflected back from the bar coded 'finger prints'.

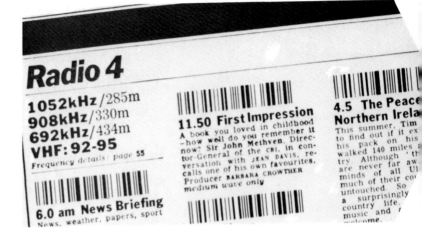

Computing the coughs

There can be few experiences more unnerving than to hear a group of doctors gravely discussing your chest X-rays.

The first holds the smudgy picture up to the light. 'Well, at least we needn't worry about the lungs. Clear as a bell.'

'No, no, my dear fellow,' says the second, 'there are patches all over. Can't you see?' and his finger stabs at the film.

'I wouldn't go as far as Charles,' says the third, 'but there's a very worrying shadow here.'

An 'expert system' in a Scottish hospital.
Left: A patient with acute abdominal pain is examined by a junior hospital doctor.
Centre: The doctor's clinical findings are systematically recorded on paper then entered into the computer in a coded form. Note the doctor's judgement '?Appendicitis' and her note of the computer's diagnosis.
Right: The computer compares the pattern of symptoms with a large number of earlier case histories and comes up with its likely diagnosis in this case, a 61% probability of appendicitis.

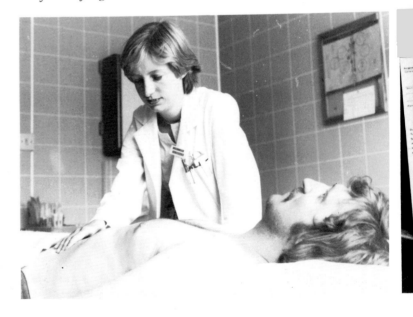

'Isn't that a rib?' asks the first. 'Anyway, who's going to Molly's tonight? It'll be quite a thrash.' And so it goes on.

The analysis of X-rays is an art. Few experts agree with each other exactly what the smudges mean, and it is a high priority in medical computing to try to use machines to make sense out of what is now mere opinion. How would the computer do this?

Firstly, it has to get the X-ray picture inside itself. This is not very difficult, using a TV camera or some other electronic

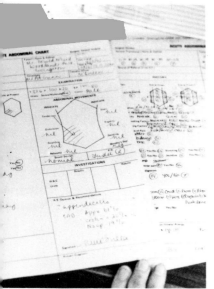

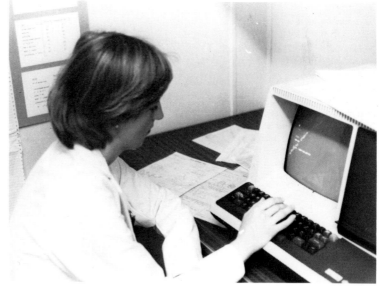

scanning device. The picture is effectively divided up into squares, small enough so that no medical feature is wholly inside any one. The intensity of the image in the square is coded as a number and stored in the computer together with details about the position of the square. This is a common procedure, generally called 'digitising' the picture. The squares that make up the picture elements are called 'picture cells' or 'pixels' for short.

Once the image is in the computer's memory, the clever work begins. The computer rushes around the picture trying to connect up areas of light and dark to form an idea of the patient's body. It will have a good deal of medical 'knowledge', so that if, for instance, the X-ray is of someone's chest, it will look for the spine – a vertical bright line. It will look for the ribs, the collar bone and the shoulder blades. It will then turn its attention to the vaguer shapes – the lungs and the heart. When all these have been identified, it can then start to make judgments about the existence or not of 'shadows'. Programming the computer to do this last part may turn out to be rather difficult, since no two doctors can agree on what is a 'shadow'. The people writing the program may work the other way round. They could show the machine a lot of X-rays of people who certainly had TB, and let the machine work out for itself, by a process of trial and error, what there is in the pictures of the sufferers that is not in the pictures of the healthy.

Of course, the problem with all these 'expert systems' (there are many others being developed) is that by definition they do not necessarily produce the same answers as a human expert. How is one to judge which is right – the human or the computer?

Diagnosis at the Toshiba Medical Centre, Tokyo.
The X-ray image on the screen is built up by the computer, which holds a three-dimensional picture in its memory of the part of the body under investigation. This is generated by a low intensity, rotating X-ray beam.

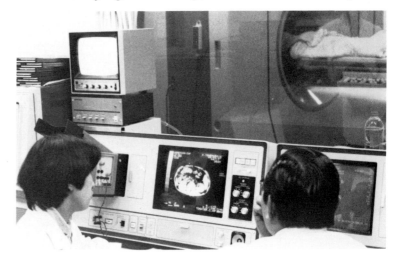

Washday wonders

If you listen to an old fashioned washing machine at work, you can hear it humming and ticking to itself – as well as thrashing the clothes around. The part that hums and ticks is a small clock which turns an elaborate series of cams which switch the various washing and rinsing cycles on and off. When your washing machine goes wrong, it is almost certainly this mechanism that has died. Modern machines will, one hopes, go wrong rather less often because they have a microprocessor controller.

What does the microprocessor controller do? Really, nothing more than the mechanical clock. It has an electronic clock that ticks away, and an electronic counter which counts the electronic ticks and therefore the passage of time. You may want to wash a load of coloured clothes. The designers of the machine have decided that to do the job properly you need a five minute prewash, a main wash with seven minutes of tumbling once the water has got to 170°F, two hot rinses of five minutes each, two cold rinses ditto and an eight minute final spin. When you press the button, or turn the dial to select the 'coloured' washing program, a program organising this sequence is selected from the microprocessor's memory. The first command turns on the prewash water, and waits for the water height sensor to report that the tub is full. Water flow is turned off and tumbling starts. A counter counts ticks until five minutes have elapsed, and then the program jumps to the pump-out routine. When that is finished water is let in again until the tub is full, the heater is turned on until the temperature reaches 170°F and tumbling starts again. It goes on until the counter has counted seven minutes worth of ticks, and then the next stage happens.

The mechanical timing mechanism from a washing machine and (right) the silicon chip whose minute electronic circuitry carries out the same logical processes (and more) with greater reliability. Of course, the chip isn't the only component in the new version, so the comparison is a little misleading.

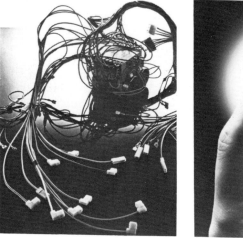

A box full of electric motors, cogs and switches is replaced by versatile electronic circuitry inside the machine. This means that the machine can do much more complicated things – if anyone wants it to – and that it can be cheaper and more reliable.

The processed word

Most people in the West now work at 'information handling' jobs, and quite a lot of them do boring, repetitive copy typing. There is no reason why a computer shouldn't help here, and this is just what a word processor – a specialised form of computer – does. Instead of typing onto paper, and then crossing out mistakes or painting them out with correcting fluid, cutting up the pages to get the paragraphs in the right order and retyping, perhaps half a dozen times, the principle of the word processor is that you type once onto a display screen, correct the mistakes on the screen and then when you are satisfied print out the result as many times as you like and store it away electronically. You can create a standard document, like a legal contract, with blanks for the names, type the names in once and print out a completely fresh personalised contract each time. Properly used, word processing saves many hundreds of hours' work.

As well as this basic function of storing text so it doesn't have to be retyped, word processors have other advantages. You can try out different line widths. You can create spaces in the text for photos or drawings. You can produce columns of figures automatically and, in some systems, do the arithmetic to create the figures. You can merge two documents together to create a third, or pull in names and addresses from a file of customers to print out form letters – each addressed to an individual.

When several people in an office are using word processors – or microcomputers running word processing programs, which is a cheaper way of doing the same thing – they can be linked together. Then, in a magazine's office, say, a reporter can write an article on his word processor and store it in the central file. The editor can call it up onto his machine to see if he likes it – and maybe change a few words, just to show who's boss. The sub-editor then looks at it on his word processor and corrects the spelling and punctuation. (He may well use a special computer program to help with this, which runs through the text, marking what it thinks are mistakes.)

When the article is tidied up to everyone's satisfaction it can be sent by telephone line to the printers and read straight into

EDITOR

their photosetting machines, so there is no need for the type-setters to do any retyping.

Word processors could have uses in most offices and when they are linked together we will have the foundation of the 'paperless office' in which people will communicate electronically. Whether that will be better or worse than today's office systems, we shall have to see.

> The number and scope of technical terms in use has grown, too. These language factors pose an entirely different challenge ** the growing difficulty of producing correctly spelled document.
>
> Rising quantities of doocuments, increasing numbers of authors, and speling complexities have combined to make information bottlenecks more likely. To make decisions, key people in your organization need timely information. The availability of timly, accurate information might very will help key people avoid making decisions based on outdated information, or take advantage of fleeting profit opportunities.
>
> Traditionally, increased information volumes have been met by hiring additional typists, placing trains on payrolls and working space. Today, increasing numbers of executives are looking for text handling and display systems to help

Bringing it all back home

As we have seen, the computer is capable of an exciting and varied range of jobs surprisingly, perhaps, since none of this is particularly new. At any time during the last 10 years, a computer pundit could have told you something similar. What is new is the fact that jobs like these can now be done – in principle, at least – by a piece of equipment small enough and cheap enough to fit onto the desk or into the pocket. Computing used to be a very expensive, esoteric resource. Now it is being brought to the masses, just as cars brought travel, the telephone and telegraph brought communication and typewriters brought printing – of a sort. The microcomputer differs from the old, big computers in that it is cheap enough to be part of an individual's personal equipment to use how he or she likes. It may be used in the home or in the office or it may dissolve the distinction between the two, putting us back into a world of cottage in-industries where people work at or near their homes with their families and friends – and their homes can be anywhere in the world, thanks to satellite communications.

Let us take a look, then, at what this versatile machine is and how it evolved. We need to delve quickly back into history to see just what computing is all about.

A little light history

In computing, *numbers* are daughters of Earth, the tools with which ingenious man gets a grip on *things*.

In the history of computing the first, and vastly the largest, step was the invention of the concept of number. Until man had a mental tool with which to represent this very odd abstract notion of the quantity inherent in a flock of sheep or a bunch of grapes or a crowd of people he could do no mathematics, no computing.

The Calculator's Progress
a) The abacus, which appeared in China in about the 13th century.
b) A replica of Pascal's calculating machine, 1642, which could add and subtract (unreliably), using a stylus to move the wheels.

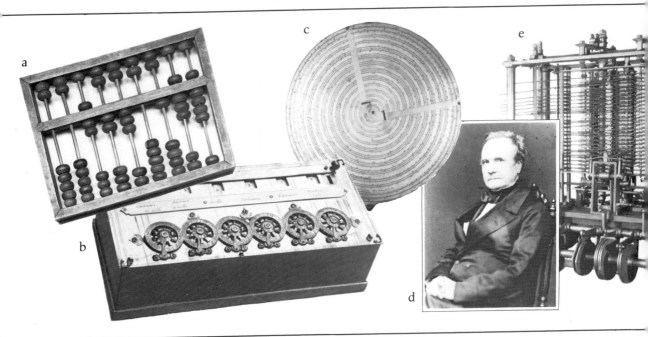

c) Henry Sutton's spiral slide rule, 1660.
d) Sir Charles Babbage (1791–1871) aimed to produce a machine which could be mechanically programmed to perform elaborate calculations.
e) A part of Babbage's 'analytical engine', designed to multiply, divide, add and subtract, and even print out an answer. It was unfinished at the time of his death.

Soon people began to invent devices to help with the manipulation of numbers. At the simplest level, if you want to know how many apples are left from a dozen when you've eaten five, you have to count on your fingers, and then if you eat one more you have to count all over again. Then some bright spark invents the device of 'subtraction' – a set of rules that can be applied to any two numbers. The idea of 'subtraction' is in essence a tool just like an adze or a plough – it increases the power of its user.

Another clever person invented symbols on paper to represent numbers and showed how to manipulate them to carry out the rules of arithmetic, which was another computing device. It is well said in mathematics today that 'mathematics is notation' – when you have invented a name for one of the sons of Heaven and a way of writing it on paper you have a grip on it, you have turned it into a tool.

The inventor of the abacus made the paper dynamic. Instead of having to write out a new line to represent each stage of the calculation, you flicked the beads about on the wires. They automatically did the boring parts of the sum, leaving you to put in the interesting parts.

f) The Gem Calculator (1890) could add up to £19.19s.11¾d.

g) The Comptograph (1900), an early commercial adding machine.

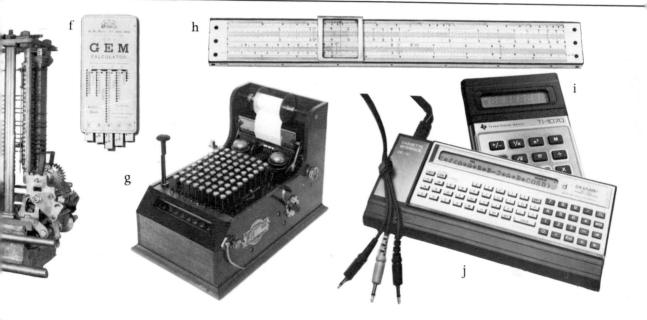

h) A mid-20th Century slide rule.
i) Pocket calculator of the late '70's.
j) Programmable calculator/computer of 1980.

The Seventeenth Century and then the Industrial Age produced many devices for automating mathematics. Most notable of these were probably those of Sir Charles Babbage – an inventive genius who is thought of as the father of the modern computer. Not long ago the calculator for the average student was a book of Logarithms or the slide rule but, only 10 years after the appearance of the mass-produced electronic pocket calculator, they now seem to be very crude and antiquated ways to automate the business of multiplication, division, raising to powers, extracting roots and doing trigonometry.

During the last War it was necessary to train all sorts of people quickly to navigate aircraft across the oceans or to calculate the fall of shells. Vast quantities of new and complicated tables were produced to automate the difficult calculations involved. They were produced by the first electronic computers – Colossus at Bletchley Park, Eniac in America and a Ferranti machine at Manchester – which consisted of electronic devices counting on their invisible fingers (hence the term 'digital computer'). These computers were also needed to decode German and Japanese military signals which had been encoded by a machine called Enigma. It replaced each letter in a signal with another letter of the alphabet, choosing the other letter in a very complicated way. The first time round 'a' might be coded as 'q', the next time as 'b', next as 'z' and then, perhaps, just as 'a'. The coding patterns were repeated at very long and unpredictable intervals; to find when the pattern repeated, it was necessary to compare each chunk of each signal with other signals in the same series in the hope that some common phrase might have been repeated at just the right point to be coded in the same way. Having discovered such a link the codebreakers could then work backwards and forwards comparing the coding of the dissimilar texts. Knowing the relative frequencies of letters in German they could often wrestle out enough information to set their own Enigma machine (or its representation in the computer) to the same code as the Germans were using at the time.

These early machines filled whole rooms with radio valves to give the calculating power of a modern pocket calculator. Because there were so many valves, one of them could be counted on to burn out every few minutes, severely limiting the time during which a program could run.

They were programmed at the crudest, lowest level, and were difficult to use. Not surprisingly a civil service committee reported after the War that there might be a use for just three or four of these machines in this country.

If the radio valve had remained the standard electronic device the computer would still be an esoteric curiosity. Happily, the transistor was invented in the late forties. Even then it had huge advantages over the radio valve for building computers: it was very much more compact, used low voltages and small amounts of power. Since then, steady improvements have been made in the way transistors are constructed.

These improvements led to the first integrated circuit, in which a number of transistors and other electronic devices, together with the wiring that connects them, are manufactured

A section of Colossus I.
the first successful electronic computer, which started work in December 1943. It was used by cryptoanalysis experts at Bletchley Park during World War II. Note the banks of valves.

The Eniac computer
also of World War II – at the University of Pennsylvania – gives an idea of
the size of these early electronic machines.

The thermionic radio valve – now almost extinct.

Single transistors of the 1950's – based on germanium.

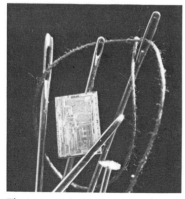

The integrated circuit – thousands of transistors on a single chip of silicon.

in one piece. Development of this technology led to the silicon chip, in which huge numbers of these devices are today packed onto a tiny sliver of silicon only about a quarter of an inch square.

The course of computing since the War has been the result of two forces. First, as transistors got smaller and more of them could be put on a chip, so computer designers used more and more of them to make the machines bigger and more powerful. Secondly, the same tendency made it possible to build a smaller and cheaper computer of the same power as those early computers. Indeed over the last decade *the real cost of computer power has halved every year.* It is now so cheap that computing can be considered a revolutionary technology. The result has been a wide range of computers. Today they fall crudely into three groups: mainframes, minicomputers and microcomputers.

The cost of computing

1950 – £1,000,000

1960 – £100,000 +

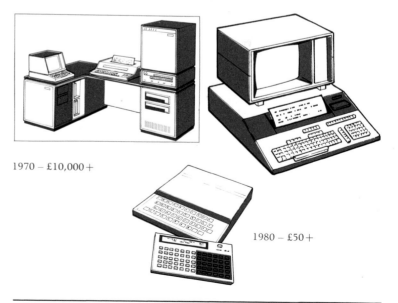

1970 – £10,000 +

1980 – £50 +

The big,
the middling
and the small

A *mainframe* computer is a large machine costing at least several hundred thousand pounds, which has to be kept in a specially constructed building and has a large attendant staff of operators, programmers and analysts. Originally all electronic computers were like this: today only a relatively small proportion are. The modern mainframe computer is a very powerful machine which can handle the very large volumes of work needed in some large companies, or very complex calculations like those required for the Inland Revenue, or the weather predictions we talked about at the start of this chapter.

In the sixties the processing capacity of mainframes outgrew the handling capacity of single input/output devices, and the techniques of 'timesharing' were introduced. A timesharing machine has a number – perhaps more than 100 – of terminals. The person sitting at each terminal has the use of the central computer for a few thousandths of a second from time to time, but the machine is so fast that it can respond to each user as if he had the sole use of the machine.

Unfortunately for the future of timesharing, the user often has to communicate with the central computer down inefficient

telephone lines – which make his access very slow. So much so that very often the user of a small personal computer will get easier and faster computing than the user of a terminal connected to such a mainframe. Since this kind of machine is designed to be used by computer professionals, it is generally quite a tough business to make it work.

A *mini* is a smaller computer, costing some £10,000 to £100,000. It may also allow timesharing, but is a less demanding device which usually does not need a special building or the services of more than a couple of specialists. Of course, it also has less power and capacity than the larger machines, but the power at its disposal is sufficient for a wide range of commercial and scientific applications.

A *microcomputer* is much smaller and cheaper again – so cheap, in fact, that each user can afford to have his own machine. Since much of the rest of the book is about microcomputers, we will not say anything more about their physical characteristics here. However, there are some things worth saying about their cultural impact.

Left: *A modern mainframe computer with enormous computing power.*

Centre: *A mini computer suitable for a medium size company.*
Right: *A micro computer with plug-in program cartridges.*
All three computers work in basically the same way.

How the microcomputer is changing the world

The appearance of the personal microcomputer, which puts an impressive amount of computing power on the user's desk, under his completely personal control, is having a profound effect on the culture of computing.

The state of computing now is very much like that of printing and book publishing at the time Gutenberg and Caxton first had their printing presses up and running. Before that, book making was a very big performance indeed. It was carried out very slowly, by hand, in monasteries, at great expense. Only dukes and kings could possibly afford to have books made and because dukes and kings spent all their time fighting in order to stay rich, many of them had no time to learn to read. When they'd got their Book of Hours or Life of St Jerome, it was of no use to them in the way we would find a book. They couldn't curl up with it for a good read by the fire before going to bed.

Of course, they didn't want books for that. They commissioned them first of all because, by doing so, they kept in with the people who controlled the actual executive power of the state. Secondly, books were commissioned because they were magical and prestigious treasures which contained the laws and scripture that controlled ordinary illiterate men's lives.

The alert reader will detect an intended similarity between this description of books and the big computer programs and installations of our day. Books were commissioned by people who couldn't read and were made in remote monasteries at vast expense. Computer programs are commissioned by managers who are unable to understand them and written in remote offices belonging to companies like IBM and ICL.

This analogy can be continued with the printing press which can put identical, cheap text into the hands of everyone who can read. Imagine Caxton printing the obvious thing – the Bible – and then some Royal proclamations and a tide table or two, and is standing at the door of his shop twiddling his thumbs and worrying about cash-flow when who should walk in but the author Mallory with the Morte d'Arthur – a cracking good yarn of tin-clad folk – under his arm, and Caxton is off into a whole new industry – book publishing.

This is very much like the computing business again. The microcomputer is like the printing press that puts computing power – literature – into every literate hand. The Bible is the obvious book to print because it has been handwritten in large numbers. There's a market for it. It corresponds to the payroll, stock control and word processing program packages that inundate the microcomputer world. However, having produced those, the microcomputer market is twiddling its thumbs, looking for something which as yet hardly exists – the computing equivalent of Mallory with a novel under his arm, and a whole new industry in the offing. In fact he is emerging here and there and no doubt in 50 years time historians will be able to point to our very own data processing Shakespeare whom nobody recognised till much later.

One can see how things were in 1477 when Caxton had just started. The monks from the monasteries were saying that ordinary people would never learn to read, that books needed individual attention and that any suggestion that a book – a real book – would ever cost less than 100,000 crowns was the most irresponsible folly. Well, the printed word and mass literacy caught on quite well, and produced many changes in the then world that no-one foresaw – among them being, perhaps: the decline of Latin, the rise of national languages and nationalism, public opinion, mass marketing, bus tickets and other advantages too numerous to mention.

There are some people who think that the mainframe computer with its hordes of salesmen, computer scientists, systems analysts and applications programmers is as doomed as the monks from the monasteries doing their gold leaf illuminated letters in the quiet cloisters at the cost of an arm and a leg a volume, for battle-hardened clients who could hardly sign an 'X' at the bottom of the contract. It will be interesting to see what changes its successor brings about in our modern world.

The old and the new Latin; incomprehensible to the layman but giving power to those in the know?

```
loop-stack pointer storage location, are set up corr
to  send  Xtal's original routines on a tour of our
the beginning of the IF...THEN statement, so we do i
By  changing  the contents of 1812 HEX to: JP INIT,
called, control first passes to a new INIT routine w
the counters and sets up the stack pointer.

    INIT.PUSH HL, DE, BC, AF
         LD DE,0E7AH
         LD HL,TABLE
         LD BC,06
         LDIR
         POP AF, BC, DE, HL
         JP Z 1416H; The jump in Xtal's RUN routine
                    which we replaced with the jump
                    to INIT
         JP 1815H;  Jump back to Xtal's RUN
    TABLE.7AH 0EH 00 00 00 00

As I said at the beginning, the purpose of this  art
```

What does it do and how does it do it?

Some people have a 'science fiction' view of computers – they think that they have an intelligence of their own, and if we're not careful, will eventually take over the universe. In fact, the opposite is true. The computer is a very stupid device. All it does is execute, with the minutest precision and at great speed, the instructions it has been given. It has no way of telling – except through further instructions written into it – whether what it is doing is sensible or foolish. It has no mind in the human sense; it has no more mind than a lawn mower.

There is 'intelligence' in what the computer does – but that intelligence is provided by its instructions, and by the human being who writes those instructions. The computer is just a tool which the human uses for carrying out his computing activities. As we saw in our quick historical review, computing is nothing new, though the electronic computer as a tool for computing is still a novelty to most of us.

What can this tool do? This depends on what we ask it to do but, basically, all its functions are built up from a few very simple activities. The most important are that it can:

add two numbers together;
subtract one number from another number;
compare two numbers or symbols to see if they're the same.

What use is that? You might well ask. In fact, a lot of use. It is because the machine can do such a tremendous number of these very simple things in a short time that it can be used for such a wide range of applications. When we come to look at the parts of the computer, we'll be able to give you some examples of this speed (see page 47).

'Canomorphic hardware with interactive anthropomorphic software' – new Latin for 'K9' from 'Dr Who?'

Building up the skills

First, one example of the way these simple operations – adding, subtracting and comparing – build up to make real-life computer applications. Remember our search for Mr Brznski (page 13)? The computer could find his telephone number by comparing his name, letter by letter, with every name in the telephone book. We're dealing with letters – so how do numbers come into it? A simple scheme might go something like the one described below.

Each letter is stored in the computer as a code number. Suppose for simplicity A is 1, B is 2 and so on. The first name in the telephone book might be 'AAA Minicabs'. The computer's program would tell it to take 'Brznski' and compare the code for its first letter (2) with the code for the first letter of the first entry (1). Its instructions would be to take each name in turn and compare the codes until the two first numbers were equal (then it would have found the Bs). Its next instruction would be to compare second letters (R might be 18) until they were identical (which might be for 'BRAACHEN') and so on, until all the word matched. Only then would it print out the result. It sounds tedious but it's actually very much like what we do when we look up a number except we don't bother with code numbers and we take short cuts because we know that B is near the beginning of the alphabet and R is two-thirds of the way down it.

This job of comparing symbols is one that the computer does frequently, particularly when it is processing text. It is unfortunate that we think of computers as being about mathematics because in real life they spend most of their time comparing parts of words to see if one is the same as another. After all, this is what our brains spend a lot of time doing. If someone says 'Meet me at the Festival Hall' you have to compare the word 'meet' with a dictionary in your head until you find the right word and discover that you are meant to 'come upon, fall in with, find' (OED). A similar procedure is used with the other words – in particular 'Festival Hall', which obliges you to look up some kind of map in your head or on paper telling you how to get there.

From time to time, mathematics is called for. The mathematical abilities of the computer have to be built up from the same simple tricks: addition, subtraction and comparison. Later, we shall see how the computer combines these operations at great speed to enable it to do very complex calculations.

From electronics to counting

You are probably wondering by now how a computer actually carries out these operations, and why it treats numbers and letters as being just the same when, to us, they are quite different. To explain some of this, we must first go back to look at electronics, and find out briefly what it means.

Electronics involves electricity. In a computer, information is sent as patterns of current down the wires and through the transistors and other devices in the electronic circuit. These patterns can change hundreds of thousands of times per second as the currents go on and off – and that is the secret of the computer's speedy operation.

In fact, the patterns make up the basis of the computer's numbering system. Each part of the pattern is called a 'bit'. We

do most of our arithmetic on a numbering system based around 10 – the number of our fingers. We count up to nine, and then use the tenth digit to 'carry one' over to the left. Using pulses of current the computer can only count up to one! In fact it has two options: a pulse of electricity, or no pulse. To the computer, that's a 1 or an 0. 0s, in this system, become very important.

It's binary!

Two real life examples of 'binary' patterns – where something can be in only one of two states. Right – each traffic light can only be 'on' or 'off'. Left – Well-disciplined Soviets hold their cards up one way or the other to create the mascot 'Mischa' at the opening of the Olympic Games in 1980.

DECIMAL	BINARY EQUIVALENT
0	0
1	1
2	10
3	11
4	100
5	101
6	110
7	111
8	1000
9	1001
10	1010
11	1011
12	1100
13	1101
14	1110
15	1111
16	10000

The numbering system, based on 1s and 0s, is called 'binary', and this is how it works. We start off just like we do in decimal counting: 0, 1. Then we have to 'carry one' to count any further, so 2 in decimal becomes 10 in binary, 3 becomes 11, 4 becomes 100 and so on. Try working out for yourself what 10100 and 110011 in binary would stand for*. The computer can manipulate these binary numbers just as we manipulate our decimal numbers, adding and subtracting them in the same kind of way. For human beings, it's hard work, though, as you will find if you try it. So you will be glad to know that, except in special cases, you should never have to use binary in talking to the computer.

*(10100 is 20; 110011 is 51).

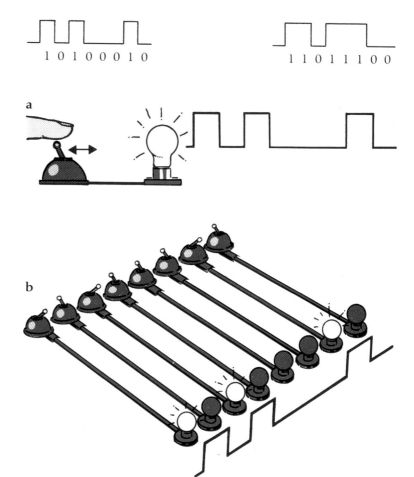

Two binary 'bit' patterns – for the numbers 162 and 220.
Inside the computer a '1' means that there is a 5 volt supply to a particular part of the circuit; '0' means no voltage at all.

Series and parallel: two ways in which binary patterns can exist in the computer.
In 'serial' form the patterns appear as a stream of 'on's' and 'off's' one after the other – rather like the pulses of current produced by the electrical circuit shown (a). In 'parallel', eight values can exist simultaneously along eight parallel circuits similar to the circuits shown (b)

1 0 1 0 0 0 1 0

1 1 0 1 1 1 0 0

As well as calculating in binary numbers, the computer also uses binary codes to represent the rest of the characters on a standard typewriter-type keyboard. In the chapter on programming (Chapter 4) we show how the computer tells which groups of 1s and 0s it should treat as characters, and which as numbers.

Some of the codes representing letters and other characters in the computer.
These are in a sense arbitrary but there is an internationally agreed convention – known as ASCII – the American Standard Code for Information Interchange.

CHARACTER	NUMBER	BINARY CODE
B	66	01000010
I	73	01001001
T	84	01010100
;	59	00111010
?	63	00111111

What is the computer made of?

All computers consist of the same fundamental parts, whatever their size:

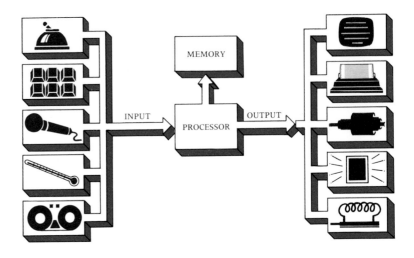

1 Input devices which take in information from the outside world and convert it in one way or another into the binary code which the computer can cope with. For example, a switch, a keyboard, a microphone or a temperature sensor – each could be an input device and the computer might have one or a number of them.

2 A memory – which can store information from outside, including the instructions which have been given to the computer. These are called its program (usually spelt with one 'm').

3 A central processor, which acts as the 'brain' and processes the information in accordance with the program of instructions.

4 Output devices which receive the messages from the computer and do something useful with them: it could be by producing messages on a television screen or a printer or operating a motor, a loudspeaker or a heater (as in a washing machine).

The memory The memory is just what it says: the place where the computer keeps information when it is not actually working upon it. We can think of it consisting of several thousand 'letter boxes' or 'pigeon holes'. Information is held there as bits of electric charge.

In a particular spot in the computer there either is a charge or there is not, so it's for this reason that computers understand binary code – 0 means no charge, 1 means a charge (analogous to morse code, except that whereas morse consists of patterns of dots, dashes and gaps, binary information consists only of patterns of dots and gaps). Some of the patterns represent numbers, as we have seen, and some can represent characters. The memory can store numbers and characters and these can be fetched by the processor. Each 'letter box' has an address, which is also a number. The processor (see below) can connect itself to any particular memory location – a particular letter box – by specifying its address.

In most microcomputers, there are 65,536 memory locations, with addresses going from 0 to 65,535. Why this exact number? The answer is that most microcomputers deal in chunks of information eight binary digits, or 'bits' long. Eight bits is called a 'byte', and has become the standard computing unit of information simply because it fits conveniently into several different uses. One reason is that you can easily code the characters of the keyboard using 255 symbols and 255 is the decimal number which is equal to 11111111, the highest number with eight digits in binary.

Two bytes, when used together as an address for the computer's memory, give $2^8 \times 2^8 = 2^{16} = 65536$ different numbers, and that is how many memory locations the ordinary microcomputer can cope with. (The obvious next step would be to have three address bytes, which would give $2^8 \times 2^8 \times 2^8 = 2^{24} = 16,777,216$ locations.)

If we think of each memory location as keeping its stored number on an ordinary postcard then all the postcards, laid end to end, would stretch out for nearly five miles.

The processor can connect itself to any one of these 65,536 boxes. It can 'write' electronically onto the card there, or 'read' back the number that was written last time, in a quarter of a millionth of a second. In other words, it can read every number in every address of its memory in a sixtieth of a second. It's this speed that makes the very simple things a computer does useful: it can do such a tremendous number of them in the time it takes you to blink.

Each individual memory location has a capacity of eight bits (in the normal system used by microcomputers). So it, too, can store numbers up to 255. If the computer needs to store larger numbers, or anything else which doesn't fit, it has to use several memory locations for each number.

We have talked about the computer using pulses of electric current to indicate its 1s and 0s and that it manages to store this information in a memory. Inside the memory the information is held as minute charges of electricity. Unfortunately, the system only works when the computer is switched on. When it is switched off, the information is lost and consequently different types of memory storage are needed to hold information which the computer needs to keep (or you, its user, need to keep) for longer than it takes to run a program. We look at these different types of memory on page 87.

The processor The processor has a lot inside, but in essence it is just like a black box which takes numbers or characters from memory and operates on them using instructions also taken from the memory, such as 'add', 'subtract' or 'compare'. After that it sends the results back to the memory or elsewhere.

A crucial feature of the processor's relationship with memory is that it can use the number stored in any location either as data or as instructions. The difference between them is quite simple: the instructions tell the computer to do something, the data is what it does it with. This gives the programmer (if he is working directly in the computer's binary codes) a great deal of freedom, and allows him, for instance, to write much bigger programs than can fit into memory at one time. He can do this by writing a small bit of program that tells the processor to take the new bits of the main program from a storage device and put them into memory. Once in the memory, they can be treated as instructions working on the data in other bits of memory.

Silicon chips We are talking glibly about the processor and the memory – but what are they? What do they look like? In a modern computer they are likely to consist of one or more silicon chips. A chip is a piece of silicon a quarter of an inch square, covered with very fine metal connections joining together thousands of transistors. It is hermetically sealed in a plastic case usually with 40 metal legs, so it looks like some sort of mechanical centipede. In today's microcomputer each memory chip generally holds 16,384 bits, so the 65,536 bytes of a complete memory takes 32 such chips.

It is important to remember that a microcomputer is the total package. It will usually consist of a board containing the silicon chips and various connecting bits and pieces. It will have a means of inputting and outputting information, from one or a number of input and output peripheral devices. It may well be as big as a couple of electric typewriters and cost anything up to

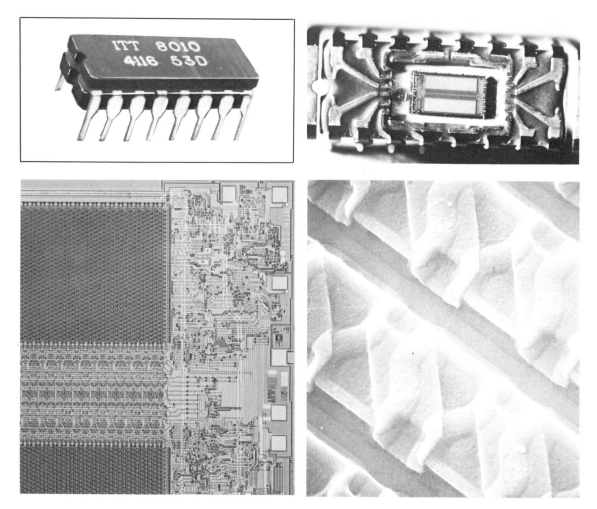

The chip exposed:
Top left: A memory chip fully
packaged (about 2 cms long).
Top right: Looking down on the
chip itself after the outer plastic is
removed. Note the fine gold wires
which connect the chip to the
centipede-like electrical connections.
Below left: Microscopic view of the
minute electrical components which
make up one quarter of the chip.
Below right: An electron
microscope's view of just a few of
the individual transistors
(magnification × 2040).

£4,000. The microprocessor in this case is just the main chip. It
weighs perhaps an ounce and costs around £5. If the microprocessor is the main chip in the typical microcomputer, it is also
possible now to produce virtually the whole microcomputer on
one single chip which contains within itself the processor and
the memory and a good deal of the input and output electronic
circuitry. Such chips have particular programs of instructions
'burned' permanently into them so that they can be dedicated to
doing particular tasks – like controlling a model train or a washing machine. The 'dedicated' microcomputer chip is likely to
find its way into a vast range of domestic, industrial and commercial equipment – from the television game to the latest tea-
vending machines to the computer in next year's car.

'Mass' or 'backing' storage.
Right: Large magnetic tapes of a mainframe computer.
Below left: A hermetically sealed 'hard disc' unit with a mini computer.
Centre: Hard discs in safe keeping.
Right: 'Floppy discs' and cassette tapes, used by a typical microcomputer.

Mass storage A most important part of a microcomputer is its 'mass' or 'backing' memory storage. This plays the same part in its organisation as a filing cabinet does in an office. You can keep programs and data in the backing store in the same way as you would keep documents in the filing cabinet. Whenever you need a particular reference you go to the cabinet and get it out on the desk. Whenever you need some information in the backing storage, you connect it to the computer so it can act as part of the machine's memory, ready for computing to be done.

Unlike the computer's internal working memory, the information kept in backing storage is retained even when the storage medium is not connected up to the computer, or when the computer is switched off. That is one reason why every computer that is going to act as more than a quick calculator needs to have some form of backing storage available. The other reason is that the computer's internal 'working' memory is not large enough to hold all the data the computer needs to work on, so it needs to be able to keep it in this external reservoir. The low-cost microcomputer uses a low-cost backing store, which is almost always cassette tape in a standard cassette recorder. The advantage of this is cheapness; the disadvantage is slowness. To get at a particular program or file of data you may have to reel through 15 minutes of tape, which is tiresome and not at all practicable for any kind of serious computing, although it's fine for the beginner who isn't in a hurry.

'Serious' microcomputers use 'floppy discs' which are rather like gramophone records covered with the same magnetic material that coats a cassette tape. The floppy disc is slotted into a disc drive where it is spun at several hundred rpm while a read/write head is moved over it from edge to centre. By putting the head in the right place, the data in that 'track' can be read in a few thousandths of a second. The floppy disc is a much more manageable way of storing data than a tape, because any chunk of data on it can be retrieved in – typically – about one-fifth of a second. 'Floppies' come in two sizes – 'mini', which store between 80,000 and 500,000 characters and 8-inch which store between 250,000 and half a million characters (remember: six characters go to the average text word).

A recent development is the Winchester or 'hard disc'. In this system the disc is fixed in the machine, which means that all the mechanical clearances can be much smaller. By this method the head can get closer and write much smaller patterns of magnetism onto the surface, and so an 8-inch hard disc can store up to eight million characters a side. Because all the clearances are so small, and therefore there's no room for dust and fluff, the disc has to be hermetically sealed. A hard disc system small enough to fit into a desk drawer can hold a maximum of 140 million characters – equivalent to about 11 years non-stop typing, eight hours a day.

Input Getting information into the computer system essentially means converting information in one form into electronic signals that can be recognised by the computer. The most popular method of getting information into a computer is through a keyboard. This bears an external resemblance to a normal typewriter keyboard, except the depression of a key causes a series of electronic pulses to be sent to the computer. The keyboard can be part of the computer housing, or a separate unit, usually with an attached video screen or a printer. In fact, the first keyboard units were based on the ubiquitous teletype that, in one form or another, provided telex links throughout the world.

A touch sensitive keyboard in a computer costing less than £100. When the keyboard is pressed, electrical contact is made between two thinly separated metal connectors as they are squeezed together.

The cheapest method of producing a keyboard is to have two layers of plastic with a conducting membrane in between. The most expensive use highly sophisticated electronic, and even ultrasonic methods.

Most keyboards have the usual 'QWERTY' layout, and are capable of producing both upper and lower case letters. Some smaller keyboards look like calculator pads, and are usually used to enter data and instructions in the computer's binary code.

There are other methods of getting information into the computer. The most obvious is to connect it up to the electrical impulses produced by the electrical or mechanical system being controlled. This is how most industrial computer systems get their information. Sensors in the system convert mechanical or environmental data – like temperature, displacement or speed – into electronic signals that the computer can deal with. We saw this type of operation in several of the applications we described at the start of this chapter – for instance, in the sensors that measured the temperature and pressure for the jet engine and the water level for the washing machine. You will recall some

INPUT

42

of the other input methods that turned up in those examples, too: the optical wand that reads bar codes, the camera that scans X-ray pictures and so on.

Another method of putting in information is by using speech recognition. We look at this (and at speech output) in Chapter 6. There are also input devices which will accept hand-writing, as

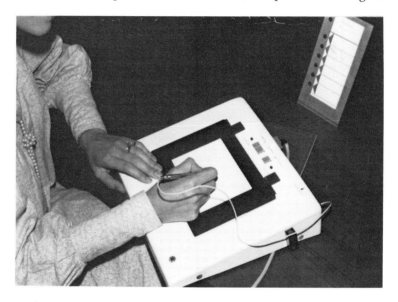

A 'graphics' tablet.
Wherever the pen touches the writing surface, detectors in both of them register exactly where it is and tell the computer the co-ordinates. It can then use the information to store or reproduce what has been drawn in some electronic form.

you write, or pre-typed or printed pages. There are 'graphics tablets' which let you draw with an electronic pen. There is also something called a 'light pen' which lets you draw on the surface of the television screen directly. You have probably heard of the punched cards, or paper tape, which were used to input information to mainframe computers. These are out of date today, however, and increasingly little used.

Output   There are just as many ways of getting information out of the computer, including many different sorts of actuators that make the computer directly control operations. For the microcomputer user the video display unit and the printer are the most common.

The video display unit
The video display unit – or VDU – can range from the domestic television set to an 'intelligent' terminal that has one or more microprocessors inside. A screen that can display 25 lines of 40 characters can hold up to 1,000 characters of information. It takes memory to store this. In so-called 'memory mapped' systems,

OUTPUT

43

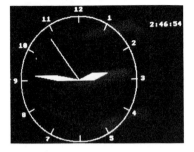

A high resolution graphics picture on the screen, made up of small picture cells or 'pixels' (reminiscent of the Russian bear on page 34).

each character position on the screen corresponds to a particular memory location in the video memory. All the computer does is transfer the contents of the memory onto the screen. As each memory location can store one byte – of eight bits – this means that 2^8 or 256 different characters are available. The codes in the memory are interpreted into actual letters and graphic symbols by a device called a character generator. Needless to say, all this memory detracts from the amount of memory available for use in the system by the user.

Another method of generating video information is to split the screen into a series of separate points, say 312×210. This requires more memory. Each point on the screen now corresponds to one bit in the memory, hence eight points require one byte of memory; 312×210 points therefore need 8,000 bytes.

This high density graphics capability is available on a number of computers. It is a useful facility for educational users and for games and hobbies but, unless complicated graphical analyses are needed, is not really necessary for business use.

Printers

There are many different types of printer available for computer users. These range from simple printers from £50 to those of a standard word processor at about £2,000.

One way of generating good quality printed output is to use a converted electric typewriter. Sometimes systems using these will allow the keyboard to be used to enter information as well.

A teletypewriter is electromechanical in construction, with a keyboard for input and an impact printer (a type cylinder) for output on paper which is stored as a roll in the machine. The speed is modest, usually 10 characters a second. Other disadvantages are that the machine is loud and usually only prints capitals. However, secondhand teletype machines can be bought quite cheaply.

Another method of producing characters on a page is by printing dots based on a 5×7 matrix. Most characters and graphics symbols can be generated in this way. The simplest dot matrix printer consists of seven needles in a vertical line that are 'fired' onto the paper as the head moves from left to right. Five such 'firings' are needed to produce each character (see p. 95). A normal typewriter ribbon means that normal paper can be used. It is possible to do quite complicated characters with dot matrix printers as each needle can be programmed individually. If the computer used has a graphics capability, a dot matrix printer must be used otherwise these characters will not be printed.

A cheap dot matrix printer capable of reproducing text and graphics. (For a diagram of how it works see page 95). This kind of printer is ideal for all but work demanding the printing of high quality text.

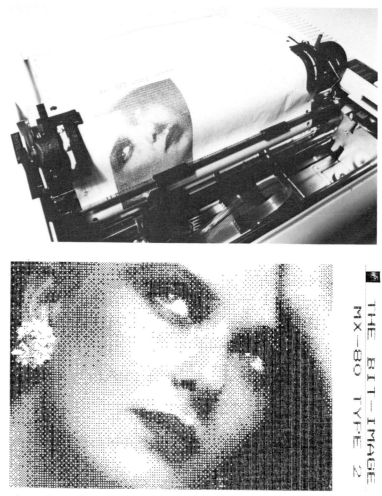

A 'daisy-wheel' printer which produces high quality print at over 100 characters per second.

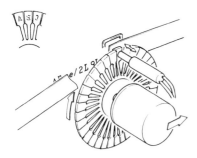

If good quality output is required then a specialised printer is necessary. The 'daisy wheel' printer is a form of impact printer that has all the characters around the rim of a circular plastic disc. A hammer hits the appropriate character to produce the printed symbol needed. These are rather expensive when compared to other sorts of printers but give good quality at high speed. The print head can be changed to give different typefaces. Most daisy wheel printers can be programmed so that right and left justification with proportional spacing is available. They are designed for word processing applications (see page 20).

All the printers mentioned use impact technology, and rely on ink coming from the typewriter ribbon to create the image on paper. They also use normal paper. There are other ways of getting image onto paper and some printers use these methods.

Heat sensitive paper is used by a number of small printers. These usually have about 40 characters per line. A small dot-matrix heating element moves across the paper and where a hot spot is created a blue dot appears on the page. They are quick and, because there is no impacting, very quiet. The paper is rather expensive, however, and is usually only available in 2-inch to 3-inch wide rolls.

Architects and designers use 'plotters', another special form of output which lets the computer draw like a draughtsman.

At the top end of the market are 'ink jet' printers which spray a fine jet of ink particles at the paper as it travels past. They are silent and very fast and many suspect that the Japanese will soon produce cheap versions to replace the more popular mechanical printers being installed in offices at present.

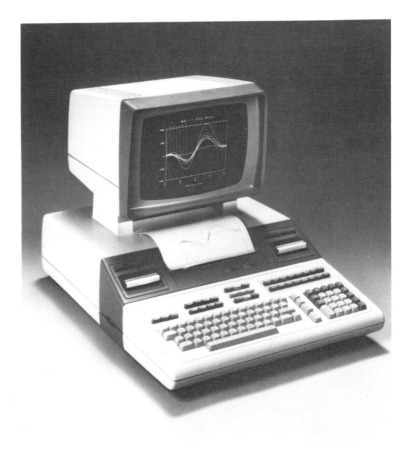

A complete 'up-market' desk-top microcomputer system.
Small plug-in cassette tapes are used to store programs and data. The high resolution graphics on the screen can be reproduced on paper using a built-in 'thermal' printer.

How fast is a computer?

So far in this chapter we have put a lot of stress on the fact that although the basic operations of a microprocessor are very simple – add, subtract and compare – its overall effect is quite clever simply because it works so fast.

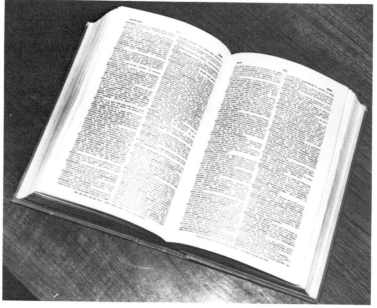

In about the time it takes for one stroke of the typewriter a small computer would be capable of searching through the electronically stored version of this dictionary, performing half a million steps.

It takes about eight seconds to multiply two 16 digit numbers together a thousand times. A typical spelling correction program would look for a word in a 25,000 word dictionary held on floppy disc, and report whether it was there or not in about one-fifth of a second. That is many times faster than a human being could do the same job. Try timing yourself. On the other hand, a human wouldn't bother to look up most of the words because he or she would know by looking at them whether they were rightly or wrongly spelt.

It is not hard for a careless programmer to squander processing power so that his program ends up taking a long time to do apparently simple things. The slowness comes because the computer spends most of its time working out what the programmer wants it to do, rather than actually doing it. However, the personal computer doesn't have to work very fast: most of the time it's waiting for its user to type something at the keyboard.

An expert typist can work at 100 words per minute: that's about 600 characters per minute, or 10 characters per second. In the time it takes to type one character the processor can carry out nearly half a million steps. However, in many cases the speed of a microcomputer is not of crucial importance. Mainframe computers cost so much that processing time – 'Mill-time' as it is called in the trade – is rather important. If your program takes too long to run you are wasting an expensive piece of capital equipment. Since a microcomputer is relatively cheap and has, usually, only one user, these considerations do not really apply. The question is: 'Would I rather do the job by hand?' and the answer is often 'No'.

What jobs can we – actual or potential users of personal computers – decide to do on our computers, though? That is a question we start to look at in the next chapter, when we consider problem solving on the computer.

2 Problems and computers

Behind each of the applications of computers we described in the last chapter there lies a problem – for example:

1 How to make sure that aircraft jet engines run at their highest power setting for take-off without overheating.
2 How to develop a cheaper, quicker way for people to find telephone numbers without having to issue every household with a fat directory.
3 How to link supermarket sales with warehouse stocking so that stock levels are kept as low as possible without ever running out of a product.

These are clearly sizeable problems for British Aerospace, or British Telecom or for Tesco's, let alone for us, so what about including some simpler problems to look at? For example:

1 How to produce something for testing a child's multiplication tables which allows the child a number of 'goes' before giving the right answer.
2 How to draw up a fixture list for local league football, so that (as far as possible) each team plays every other team – both at home and away – and the teams play at home and away alternate weeks, each team having a fixture every week.
3 How to tune a piano.
4 How to find the best route between London and Godminster.
5 Controlling a greenhouse.

Perhaps the computer could help in all of these – we shall see. However, we shall start not by looking at the computer at all but at the nature of the problems and at the ideas and techniques of problem solving. Then we shall see if the computer fits in and in a later chapter go on to solve one or two of the problems with the aid of the computer.

What do they have in common, that makes us describe them as problems? Not very much, you may think. But they do all have three basic elements:

1 We have some basic facts about each problem, which define it, make it unique. We understand, at least broadly, just what the problem is. Take that first problem, for instance. We already know we're talking about:

jet engines
aircraft take-off

the need for the highest possible power setting
the need for safety
the danger of overheating.

2   There may not always be one perfect answer which completely solves the problem.

3   There is a gap between the problem and the answer. We don't already know the answer, or there wouldn't be a problem. Sometimes, admittedly, the gap is so small that we hardly think of the problem as a problem at all. It may be a problem to choose the best route to Godminster, but it's not difficult to choose the route we'd take to call on our next door neighbours. Or is it? We might go from our front door to their front door, our back door to their back, or even squeeze through the hole in the fence. If we're planning to burgle them, we might opt to go through the kitchen window. Perhaps even that problem takes a bit more thought than first seems likely?

Solving the problem

So much for the problem – what of solving it? In everyday language we use the word solution to mean two quite different things.

1   Sometimes we mean the answer to a problem. So, the solution to a crossword puzzle clue is the word we write down in the puzzle; the solution to an arithmetical problem is the number we come to when we have worked it out.

2   Sometimes we mean the way of finding the answer. In this sense, we have solved the problem when we have discovered how to reach the answer. Getting the answer – putting the solution into practice – is a quite different step.

To avoid confusion in this chapter we shall only use solving and solution in the second of these two ways: to mean the working-out of how to reach the answer.

    Bearing this in mind, what are the steps involved in problem solving, and *how* can the computer fit in? They are as follows:

1   First there is a *problem* – sometimes you may feel you understand the problem completely – perhaps you are quite clear how to tune a piano, for instance. With other problems, you won't have a clue where to start.

2   The next step is to *analyse the problem* – make sure you know what it consists of. We shall look at this in more detail later in the chapter.

THE PROBLEM

3 Then we have to *solve the problem* – work out how to reach the answer.

4 Next we *carry out the solution* – carry out the calculations, test a possible answer to see if it works.

5 Finally, we come to the *answer* – and we don't have a problem any more.

What can the computer do?

We can rule the computer out of stage 1 – the problem – straight away. With any luck the computer is helping to solve our problem, not creating one! But can the computer analyse the problem? Basically, the answer is no. This is a piece of hard work you have to do for yourself.

The computer is also not able to solve problems in the sense in which we're now using the word 'solve'. You have to solve the problem yourself, work out how to get to the answer. Then you tell the computer this, in the form of a program; what the computer does is carry out your solution and provide the answer for you. Not very impressive, you may think. But it can be enormously helpful in some circumstances:

1 If the problem is a routine one, which you solve in the same way repeatedly – you might do the same calculation frequently on different figures or use the same technique to find many different phone numbers.

2 If the solution is simple, but carrying it out is slow or difficult – you know how to do a maths problem, but the particular numbers in this one make the calculations cumbersome; you know how to set about finding a phone number, but the size of the directory makes looking it up a slow job.

3 If carrying out the solution is, quite simply, impossible for humans – it may need to be done too quickly, or in nasty conditions, or the inevitable mistakes which humans sometimes make might lead to major disasters. Think, for instance, of the problem of reacting in time to changes in a chemical process reaction, or to the cooling system of a nuclear reactor.

It is therefore people who solve problems. Computers are a tool for helping them carry out the solutions. Now we'll look, in turn, at three aspects of this use of the computer to help people solve problems.

First the analysis of the problem: deciding what it's all about, and selecting or discovering a solution. Secondly, we'll review the kinds of solution that computers can carry out. Then in Chapter 4, we'll look at programming, the way in which people tell computers how to set about carrying out that solution.

Looking at the problem: analysis and solution

Why can people alone solve problems, and not computers? Simply because people alone can think. Computers, whatever their other uses, can't think for themselves, and problem solving involves a great deal of thinking.

All the same, many people don't think of themselves as good at solving problems. Ask them how they found a solution, and they might say:

'It's common sense, isn't it?'
'Oh, I've a sixth sense for these things.'

You may not need special training to solve many of the problems you come across day by day: they solve themselves, almost without your realising. However, you do need to be trained to set about solving the difficult ones. These need a bit more thought, and our purpose is to show you some ways of channelling and structuring that thought.

That is what analysis is all about: thinking about a problem, but in a structured way. What structure? Well, it all depends on 'what problem'! But since we've already introduced the start of a structure, we'll use that. It consists of the three parts we saw that every problem has: the facts, the answer, and the gap.

What are the facts?

It's a help to make a note of all the facts we already have about our problem. Why? Because that's a good way of finding out if we have enough facts. Do we know enough about each fact? Are there vital facts we don't have at all?

We'll take a couple of our problems. See what facts we have, and what facts we will need.

The fixture list
What do we already know? We know we're talking about a football league, but how many teams are there? Clearly we must find that out. Let's say there are 10 of them: that will mean 18 games (one at home and one away with every other team) for each team.

We know we're talking about the fixtures for one season. How many dates is that? Let's say our league plays on Sunday afternoons. Ideally, the season will consist of 18 Sundays, but if we can't schedule matches to fit in like that, we could extend it by, say, two Sundays. So we have a maximum of 20 dates on which matches could be played.

Is there going to be one right answer to the fixture list problem? Probably not. There are dozens of lists we could end up with. But some will be better than others. Let's think for a moment about which one we want.

Well, it is absolutely essential that each team should play each other team at home and away. We would therefore reject any answer in which that didn't happen. However, if there are lots of lists in which this happens, what else would we be looking for? We've already mentioned two other features which, though not essential, are very desirable: that the teams should play at home and away on alternate weeks, and that each team should have a fixture every week. To decide just which answer we want, we'd have to decide how these compare in importance.

Suppose that we're prepared to go up to our 20 date limit to the season, in order to ensure that the home and away matches are well distributed. However, if we can distribute them evenly over an 18 or 19 week season, that would be preferable.

Are there any other factors to be considered? We might, for instance, want to think about how far the teams have to travel to away matches, or in what order they play teams from the top and bottom halves of last year's league table. Do we want these facts at this stage, then? On the whole, probably not. Let us first see if we can find a list which meets the guidelines we've already chosen. Then if there are several which do, we'll think about whether it's worthwhile getting more sophisticated in our solution, to choose between them.

Route finding

The example we are using here – how to get from London to Godminster – is an imaginary one, with imaginary places on the way, like Camford and Little Wittering. In real life we might be trying to develop an enormous data bank of information which would enable, say, a travel agent to help tourists to decide how to get from place to place right across the country. Some of them might want the quickest route, some the cheapest, others the prettiest, or the prettiest provided it is not too expensive, or the fastest provided that they don't have to fly, and so on. Our example is a simple one designed to show, in principle at least, how we might go about solving the problem of creating such a route-finding aid.

LITTLE
TWITTERING

Returning to the business of setting out what we know about the problem, what alternative routes are there? What alternative forms of transport? The form of transport we choose will, naturally, affect the routes available to us. Assuming, though, that there are just three possibilities: plane, train and bus (or combinations of them), we might end up with the following:

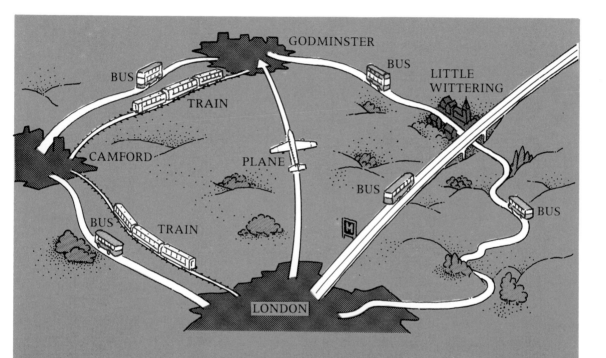

ROUTE NUMBER		FARE (£)	JOURNEY TIME (HRS)
1.	TRAIN (VIA CAMFORD)	8.00	1.50
2.	BUS/TRAIN (VIA CAMFORD)	7.50	2.20
3.	TRAIN/BUS (VIA CAMFORD)	6.50	2.30
4.	BUS (VIA CAMFORD)	5.00	3.00
5.	PLANE	10.40	1.00
6.	BUS (VIA LITTLE WITTERING)	6.00	2.50
7.	BUS (VIA LITTLE WITTERING)	5.50	2.30

These are some possible routes:

1 Train to Camford then train to Godminster.
  Bus to Camford then train to Godminster.
3 Train to Camford then bus to Godminster.
4 Bus to Camford then bus to Godminster.
5 Plane from London to Godminster.
6 Bus from London to Little Wittering by the short but boring motorway route then on by bus to Godminster.
7 Bus via Little Wittering by the slow but pretty route.

The 'best' route depends on what you are looking for. Does it matter if it is short or long? Are we most interested in whether it is cheap or quick? Is there anything we want to do on the way – like visit the Norman church at Little Wittering?

Certainly we want to know the cost of the route and the time it will take. The length of the route may not be so important.

There's no right answer to this problem, either. But there is a best answer, depending on what we are looking for. Let's look for two different 'best routes':

1 The quickest route costing £7 or less.
2 The cheapest route which takes less than two and a half hours.

We might add that although these are the most important things, if two routes come out equally on test, then we'd prefer travelling by train to travelling by bus and would like to go by plane most of all.

Filling the gap So far so good; we have the facts, and we know what sort of answer we're looking for. Now for the next bit: filling the gap between the problem and the answer.

Remember, we're not going to bring in the computer yet. We're still at the stage of analysing the problem, finding out what it consists of. Then we're going to go on to solve the problem; it's only when it comes to carrying out the solution that we'll think about whether we want to use a computer or not. So we'll go back to our two problems, and see what's in that gap.

The fixture list
We've got, on the one hand, the teams and the dates. And, on the other hand, the features we want our fixture list to have.

What's in between? The difficulty of finding a list which meets our guidelines as closely as possible. That's the gap; the solution is the way we're going to discover of finding that list.

Route finding
For this exercise, we have our routes on the one hand and our guidelines for which route we'd choose on the other. And in the middle? The job of testing the alternatives, to see which one fits the bill.

Complications

Using the methods above we've analysed our problems. Of course, these are pretty simple problems, and they haven't been too difficult to analyse. In real life, we come across some much more complex problems, not just the kind of problems we put at the head of our list at the start of the chapter (controlling the jet engine, and so on); they are pretty simple as problems, though solving them is not so easy. But what about

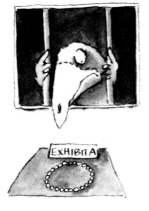

EXHIBIT A

predicting the likely sales of a new product
designing a hospital
solving the crime problem?

Difficult as these may be, it does help to go about them in the same way. The most daunting problem looks more manageable if you take a systematic look at the facts, the sort of features you want to find in your answer and at the difficulties which lie in the way between you and the answer. If you feel you can't grasp the problem at all, it can be a help to divide it up into different parts, and to analyse these one by one. We'll talk later in the chapter about some of the things you will need to look out for in doing this sort of complicated analysis.

Solving the problem

All the analysis in the world, however, won't actually solve the problem. We must now go on to the next stage: finding a solution. We're not talking about an answer, remember: just a solution, a way of reaching the answer.

The logical
and the lateral

Perhaps we should draw a distinction, first of all, between two quite different ways of going about problem solving. First, there's the logical approach. You know what you're looking for. You know what alternatives are available and you can solve the problem by looking at each of the alternatives in turn, seeing how they measure up to your objectives. You have probably already decided that this is how you'd tackle the route-finding problem. You'd calculate how much time each route took, how much each cost, and then you'd check all the routes against each other to see which one best fits the bill. There are only seven possible routes we've given ourselves, so that wouldn't take too long: there's no point in trying anything fancier.

What about that fixture list problem, though? How many possible ways are there of combining those teams into a fixture list and how are we going to find one which meets the guidelines we've drawn up? This time, there are thousands of alternatives. You would immediately rule out some which obviously don't obey our rules – those which schedule exactly the same matches week after week, for instance. But it would take a very long time to look at each possible list in turn, discard all those which won't do and list all those which will.

You may ask, isn't that what the computer is supposed to be good at – sorting through a lot of information, and fishing out the bits we want? Well yes, it is. But take a look at just how much information it would have to sort through in this case. How many ways could the list actually be made up – so that each week, let's say, each team had one match and every team was listed? For each week, that would mean 30,240 possibilities.

Then we'd have to combine the weeks with each other to make a season of 18, 19 or 20 weeks. Looking at the 18 week seasons alone (and our solution might not even come among these), there are millions of alternatives. If we now take account of the different ways of combining weeks to make up a season, the possibilities increase still further. Even for the computer to draw up all those lists and check to see if each in turn was what we were looking for, it would take a very long time indeed, even if it were working at the enormous speeds we talked about in the last chapter.

So you think there's an easier way? Well, just you find it; have a few tries, and you'll soon discover it's not that easy. In fact, it is not going to be a totally logical process at all. We'll have to make a guess at a way which might do, then test it out to see if it works – and if it doesn't, think again.

In other words, we're back to that 'sixth sense' business which we sometimes call lateral thinking – not plodding forwards logical step by logical step, but making jumps all over the place so as to cut corners. It isn't entirely magic, though. We have clues to help us. In this case, we all probably know some simple techniques for sorting information which we might use to get started. We might, for instance, decide to look at the first half of the season first, and try and fit one match between every combination of teams into the first ten weeks. Then we could use a 'mirror image' for the second half of the season. What other techniques would you try?

In fact, logical and lateral thinking aren't completely different; they merge into each other, and this kind of example – where we could deal with a few alternatives logically but need to find a different way of dealing with a lot – shows us just how they can fit together. It shows us, too, that the computer doesn't do away with the need for lateral thinking. Its speed and accuracy certainly make logical thinking a very powerful tool but there are still plenty of situations in which logic alone isn't enough.

There are other ways of thinking laterally, too, which come in handy when we have other kinds of problem to solve. We'll take a look at some later in the chapter.

We should also mention another way in which the computer cuts down the need for thinking of both kinds. We might solve our fixture problem by 'borrowing' a solution – in the form, perhaps, of a computer program someone else had written to solve a similar problem. It needn't be a football fixture problem they had tackled; it might be, say, a tennis club round robin contest, or even a timetable or a way of sorting scientific results. Football isn't the important part, when it comes to solving the problem; that's the context of the problem, rather than the content. We need a solution with a similar content, even if it occurs in a different context.

In order to find one, we need to get used to the idea of separating the content from the context – the sort of problem it is, from the details which make it unique. In this case, the content of our problem involves a way of drawing up and testing alternatives, when there are too many alternatives to work through them all one by one. We'll come across this same content in problems and solutions from very different contexts.

Mapping out the logic
Before we talk about clues and tricks to help us think laterally, let's look at the business of solving problems logically. And this is the point at which we're going to introduce flow charts.

Some people have the idea that flow charts are something special to do with computing. Not so they don't involve computer programming at all. They are simply a way of drawing up a map of our solution: planning out logically, step by step, how we're going to carry it out.

There are a number of conventions people use in drawing flow charts, but for now we're going to stick to a very simple version. It has:

a beginning – which we make this shape: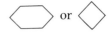

instructions on what to do next, this shape:

junctions – leading to paths which we travel down in different directions, depending on the signposts on them. We might also think of these as decision points.

They are this shape: ◁▷ or ◇

An end, the same shape as the beginning.

Joining these shapes up are paths, with arrows to show which direction we should travel along them, and sometimes signposts – often based on 'yes' and 'no' answers to questions.

We'll make all this clearer by taking a problem, and drawing a flow chart of its solution. We won't start with one of the two we've been analysing. Instead, let's take a very simple one: tuning a piano. How do you go about tuning a piano? Like this:

Piano tuning.
Once one note is tuned accurately to the pitch of a tuning fork, other notes are then compared by ear. The tuning pegs, which control the tension in the strings, are held in position by friction and a special key is used to ease them round.

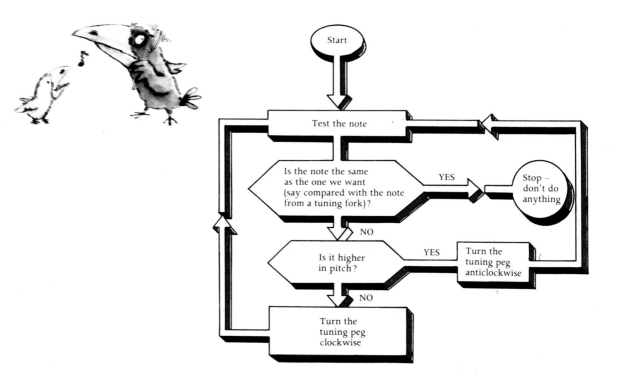

It's quite simple but have a good look to make sure you understand how it works before reading on. You'll see that though you start at the start and end at the end, you don't necessarily go down all the paths in between: only the ones you need. You may also go down some several times. The 'loops' we've put in send you backwards, so that you can repeat the operation of testing and adjusting as many times as are necessary. Loops are a very important idea in drawing flow charts and in computing programming. It is very important to make sure there is a way of escaping from these loops, so that you don't travel endlessly round in circles. How do we escape here?

Now you've got the idea, how about having a go yourself at the London to Godminster problem? Start by plotting a way of finding that first 'best route' – the quickest one costing under £7. And when you've drawn the flow chart, carry out the operations in your head to see if it works.

We've drawn our own version on the next page. Your chart need not be exactly like ours to be right. There are several right ways of solving this problem – the main thing is to make sure that yours works. Did you miss anything out? Could you escape

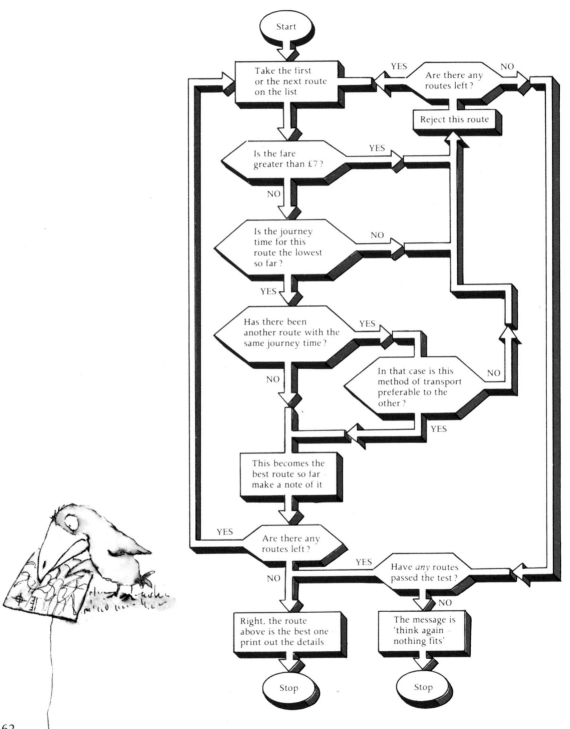

Start

Take the first
or the next route
on the list

Are there any
routes left? — YES / NO

Reject this route

Is the fare
greater than £7? — YES

Is the journey
time for this
route the lowest
so far? — NO

Has there been
another route with the
same journey time? — YES

In that case is this
method of transport
preferable to the
other? — NO / YES

NO

This becomes the
best route so far –
make a note of it

Are there any
routes left? — YES / NO

Have *any* routes
passed the test? — YES / NO

Right, the route
above is the best one
print out the details

The message is
'think again –
nothing fits'

Stop

Stop

from any loops you used? Once you're sure it is right, then you can think about whether you could have got there more simply or easily. A similar technique could be used for the alternative problem – finding the cheapest route which takes under two and a half hours.

Exhausting the possibilities

You may feel that the flow chart was pretty complicated, for such a simple problem, but we haven't put anything into the flow chart that wasn't in the original problem as we analysed it. It just shows that when you buckle down to it, there's a lot more to even the simplest problem than you first imagine. Even if you were simply looking at the map and making calculations in your head or on a scrap of paper you will, without realising it, have gone through those steps yourself. In Chapter 1, we looked at the way a computer is thoroughly stupid. It can't do anything for itself; you, the programmer, have to tell it to do every single thing. In order to tell it accurately, you really do have to be as exhaustive as this. You can imagine what the flow chart would look like for a really complicated problem!

This is not the only direction in which you need to be exhaustive in problem solving, however. You will only get the right answer if you ask the right questions; before you even draw up the flow chart, you should make sure you have taken into account all the possible solutions. We cut the alternative routes from London to Godminster down to seven, for the sake of the example, but did you take into account the possibility that none of them would fit the bill, for instance? In real life, you don't want to cut down until you have opened up. What, for instance, if the most attractive way to get to Godminster had been by canal boat? That's a possibility we didn't even consider!

Now you've seen just how much work goes into solving even a simple problem, you should be in a much better position to appreciate how much work will be wasted unless you carefully analyse every aspect of the problem before you even think about the solution.

Data and instructions

You will have noticed that when we drew the flow chart for the route finder, we didn't put any details about the routes themselves into it. We didn't even say there would be seven of them, and we could have used the same flow chart if there were 100 or 1,000.

To understand why we didn't, we need to introduce a very important distinction: between instructions and data. What are they? Well, broadly speaking:

1 Instructions are what we do, or tell the computer to do.
2 Data is what we carry out the instructions upon.

So, in this case, the instruction is the flow chart; and the items of data are the facts we found out about the routes. Much the same is true of the piano tuning example: here, the instructions are in the flow chart again, but the data are the various notes, right or wrong.

However, it's not quite so simple because what are instructions in one instance can be data in another. Let's take a fairly straightforward example. We've put our price limitation – that '£7 or less' – into the flow chart. Alternatively, we might have put it into the 'data' section. Our instructions, instead of saying, 'Is the cost £7 or less?,' might have said, 'Find the maximum the client is prepared to pay. Is the cost less than that?' You will see that this could be a very useful refinement if, say, the problem was being solved by a travel agent with lots of customers who had different budgets. So we could modify the flow chart to allow for this new instruction. Notice the new shape which means 'take in data at this point'. The modification has, of course, lengthened the flow chart.

Generally, you will find this true of instructions, whether they are in the form of flow charts, computer programs or whatever. 'Tailor' them to fit the problem precisely and they will be short and simple. Make them 'off the peg' and you will have to make them a bit bigger, but that leeway will pay off if you can use the same solution to deal with lots of different problems. It's rather like the content and context distinction we made earlier: we are taking more and more of the 'context' out of the solution and finding that the universal 'content' which is left can be applied in more and more instances.

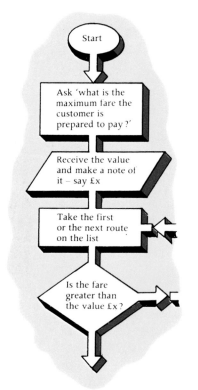

Start

Ask 'what is the maximum fare the customer is prepared to pay?'

Receive the value and make a note of it – say £x

Take the first or the next route on the list

Is the fare greater than the value £x?

The child's multiplication table

We'll take one more problem, and look at the instructions and data question for that, too: the problem of testing a child's knowledge of the multiplication tables. We need to stop somewhere so let us cut it down to the range from 1 × 1 to 12 × 12. We need to generate questions from that range and we need to test answers to see if they are right, giving the child another go if he or she gets it wrong.

1 x 5 = 5
2 x 5 = 10
3 x 5 = 15
4 x 5 = 20
5 x 5 = 25
6 x 5 = 30
7 x 5 = 35
8 x 5 = 40
9 x 5 = 45
10 x 5 = 50
11 x 5 = 55
12 x 5 = 60

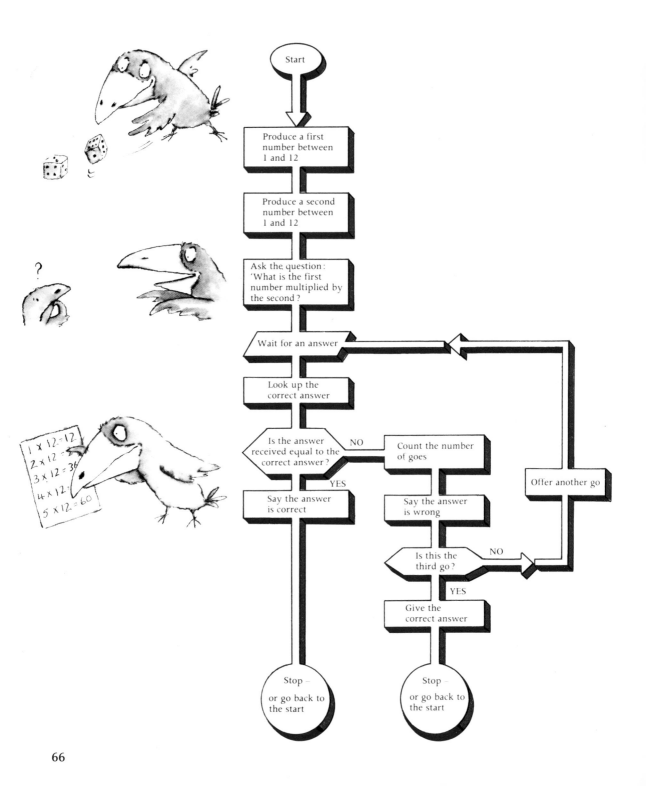

Start

Produce a first number between 1 and 12

Produce a second number between 1 and 12

Ask the question: 'What is the first number multiplied by the second?'

Wait for an answer

Look up the correct answer

Is the answer received equal to the correct answer?

NO — Count the number of goes

YES

Say the answer is correct

Say the answer is wrong

Offer another go

Is this the third go?

NO

YES

Give the correct answer

Stop —

or go back to the start

Stop —

or go back to the start

1 × 12 = 12
2 × 12 =
3 × 12 = 36
4 × 12 =
5 × 12 = 60

We want a method of producing questions and testing answers, then to ask a particular question – say, what is 6 × 8 ?, take in the child's answer and get back a 'right' or 'wrong, try again' response. After three wrong guesses we want to be able to give the right answer and then be in a position to ask the next question.

The solution   Can we solve this logically ? Yes. There are only a modest number of possible questions in the multiplication table (144, to be precise), and it should be possible to find a way of carrying out a straightforward logical solution. So let's set out the flow chart. What are the instructions here ? Simple – they're on the flow chart. But what are the items of data ? The answers given by the child are certainly data. But is there any other data ? What about two other pieces of information – the numbers we produce at the start, and the right answers ?

It depends very much, in fact, on how we carry out the solution. What do we mean by that ? Well, let's say we do all this by hand. We generate random numbers by throwing a dice, and we check the answers against a written multiplication table. Would you agree that the numbers on the dice, and the written table, are not instructions but data ?

If we program the solution for a computer, though, we'd get those numbers, and check the answers, in quite a different way. Some computers have a program to generate random numbers, and we might simply instruct the computer to dig out two 'random' numbers. All digital computers can do multiplication so that when it comes to finding the right answer, we just instruct the computer to multiply the two numbers together. Now are those numbers instructions or data ?

Not so easy, as you can see. Broadly speaking, when we are talking about a computer program, we mean by instructions what is actually written in the program; and by data what are items of information the computer has to obtain from outside the program, when carrying it out, or running it. The computer doesn't obtain anything when finding the right answer, so that's part of the instructions. Does it obtain anything when producing the numbers ? If it uses a random number generator which is part of its programming instructions (we'd just tell the computer, 'generate any number between 1 and 12), that's also part of the instructions. It would be data, however, if (for instance) we fed in a list of numbers and asked the computer to run down the list, asking one question after another. We look at this question again (and point out an important exception) in Chapter 4.

Though we've been going through our problem solving step by step – from the analysis to the solution and now to carrying out the solution – you'll have realised that it isn't as simple as all that. We have to keep looking backwards and forwards. For instance:

1 In finding the facts, we have to anticipate what kind of answer we shall want.
2 In deciding what kind of answer we want, we have to bear in mind the difficulty of solving the problem.
3 In solving the problem, we have to take into account how we're going to carry out the solution.

That last flow chart we drew is already half way to carrying out the solution – because in putting in the sources of data, we had to decide whether we were going to carry out the solution by hand or on the computer. In fact, even before listing the instructions on the flow chart, we need to know how the solution will be carried out.

Why? Well, take for instance that 'produce a random number' instruction. We need to know how it will be done before we know if it is an adequate instruction. What if we're going to carry out the solution on a computer that doesn't already have a random number generator? Then we'd have to be even more exhaustive in our instructions, either by telling the computer exactly how to generate random numbers, or by giving it a list of numbers to work down, as we suggested above.

The patterns of travel down a flow chart are closely related to the pattern of movement around a computer program. The computer, like us, will be able to 'loop' back on itself, or 'branch' down one path or another, depending on a particular result. If it couldn't we'd have to take that into consideration when we drew the flow chart and think of another way of mapping the instructions.

It's true to say, in fact, that deciding what tools we'll use to carry out the solution is still part of the solution, rather than part of the carrying-out.

Choosing the computer

Inevitably, to make our examples simple enough to be readily understandable in this chapter, we've made some of them so simple that they could easily be done by hand. Why bother to use a computer for testing the multiplication table, you may be asking yourself? I could easily act as the tester myself! However, the computer could score over doing it by hand in all the cases we've mentioned. Look at them in turn, and see what are the advantages of doing it on the computer.

Route finding: sorting and selecting

It is no problem selecting the best route manually when we've only given ourselves seven routes, and only a few simple conditions to fulfil. What if we'd investigated fully (as we'd certainly do in real life) and found a selection of routes – road, rail and air – interlocking and combining in various ways, to produce dozens of alternatives? What if we knew a dozen facts about each which might influence our choice? It would soon become extremely difficult to work through and find out which route suited us best. What if we requested a route with features that no route had? Maybe we'd ask for a route that took under two hours and cost less than £6. We'd check every one on the list, find that none fitted the bill, then decide that we'd like to know how quickly we could get there for £6? or how much it would cost if we only had two hours to spare? Change your mind dozens of times, and the computer will still be there, replying politely and never missing a vital stage through sheer exasperation.

Working at high speed, on lots of alternatives, the computer proves to be an expert at sorting information to find the particular example or examples which meet various criteria – not only routes, but names and addresses (select out, say, all the members of a particular committee from the address list of a club or association), hotels, restaurants, holidays (We want to go to Ibiza – but then we wouldn't mind Crete. What's really important is that we can't afford more than £200, and we must have a double room; we want to be able to skindive; do you think we could do that more cheaply in Corsica?; we'd skip the double room if it saved us £10, of course), etc. If the information is there, then the computer can sift through it quickly, without losing its temper – *always assuming it's been programmed correctly*.

The fixture list: working out the difficult

If you tried to draw a flow chart for this, and you are not an expert mathematician or logician, it probably drove you round the bend. Try to draw up the fixture list itself, and you'll settle after the first five hours for a half decent version. Never mind the alternate homes and aways – at least all the matches fitted in somewhere.

Can you do it on a computer? Yes, of course. It's not a program you will be writing for yourself next week, but people have written programs to deal with this sort of problem, and all you have to do is buy a suitable one or have one modified.

The multiplication table: patient teaching

Sure, you could sit for hours and fire questions at a child. But you have to be there to fire them. You have to keep concentrating and woe betide you if you give the wrong answer.

The computer never gets tired, and is always available, always accurate. It's polite even when the answers get really silly. And it's fun to use . . . for a while. Of course, a simple program like the one we've just described does no more than test. It cannot *teach* and it cannot fathom out *why* you get the wrong answer or help you get the right one. But a much more sophisticated program could do a good deal of this.

Piano tuning: sensing the unlikely

To think of the computer as a tool for piano tuning needs a fair bit of imagination, of lateral thinking. We get so readily trapped in the predictable pattern of solving familiar problems in a particular way that it takes a real effort to make ourselves see them differently. However, when you think about it, the computer could make an ideal piano tuner.

If we strip away the context of piano tuning and look at the content, the problem ceases to be about music at all. It has to do with testing and adjusting and, from Chapter 1, you will remember that sensors can act as input and actuators as output to enable the computer to test something and alter it if necessary.

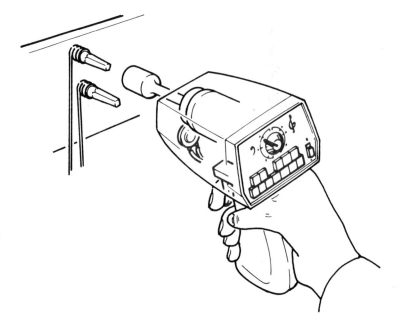

An artist's impression of a possible electronic hand-held piano tuner.
It contains a microphone, to listen to the note; a keyboard, to choose the note being tested and the octave; a special motor, geared down enormously to provide the right amount of 'twist' to turn the pegs, and a trigger to set it going.

The electronic piano tuner

A teacher from Bury St Edmunds wrote to the BBC after watching a programme about microelectronics to say that he and his wife find it difficult to find piano tuners in their area and he suggested the idea of an electronic piano tuner which would be rather like an electric hand drill in size. This would fit over the square ended tuning pegs on the piano. A microphone would pick up the sound as the string is struck and the computer would compare the frequency of the note it hears with a frequency stored in its memory. If the note were too low it would instruct the motor to tighten the string; if too high it would relax it by turning the tuning peg the other way.

In a recent programme in the television series *Managing the Micro*, Bill Davies, of Brighton Technical College, produced a mock-up of such a system and showed that it could work – at least in principle.

Clearly, a practical piano tuner would need to be mechanically very strong and extremely sensitive. It would also need to hold many notes in its memory and would need a keyboard of its own into which the user would enter the name of the note he wanted to tune.

Right: *Bill Davies designing a working electronic mock-up.* Note the small 'stepper' motor, fitted with a pointer.
Left: *Testing the equipment.* Although the motor does not have enough power to turn the pegs, it does respond correctly to the computer's signals and can tell the operator – by its movement (or lack of movement) – when the note is in tune.

Professional piano tuners say that tuning pianos is a very subtle business and doubt if a device of this kind would be good enough. However, it is amusing to speculate that one day it might become sophisticated enough to beat the human being!

The X factor: hitting the right solution

The unlikeliness of the piano tuning example underlines the importance of 'lateral thinking' – looking at the unobvious. Clearly it is important not only in selecting the method by which we will solve a problem, but also in choosing our tools.

Let's take a brief look at some of the ways in which our thinking is restricted, and at some tricks for lifting those restrictions and showing us new possibilities.

The professional touch

All of us have various thinking and operating techniques which we use in our jobs – a mixture of viewpoint and practice. Imagine asking a mathematician, an engineer and a housewife to design the perfect house. How would their solutions differ?

You'll probably agree that each would over-emphasise some features of the design, and under-emphasise others. The housewife would know a great deal about how to make a house pleasant to live in, but she might not take into consideration the location of the plumbing pipes. The mathematician might care about the proportions of the rooms, but fail to notice that the kitchen and dining room were at opposite ends of the building. The engineer might design a house that functioned perfectly from a technical point of view, with all its systems well thought out, but that just didn't look right.

Of course we need to make full use of the experience we already have in problem solving. At the same time, we need to be wary of giving too much emphasis to the familiar aspects and ignoring other important considerations. If, say, you asked a musician to find a new way of tuning a piano, do you think he would think of using a computer?

Stripping out the context

We've already mentioned the difference between the content and context, and how the context of a problem can blind us to its content. When solving that fixture list problem, for instance, it is no help to think about other aspects of running a football team. Instead, we need to compare it with other problems that involve arranging data in a particular way.

One useful way to set about this is to rephrase the problem, or even a single word in it. Suppose, say, your problem is

deciding where to put a bath. Why not get rid of the word 'bath' altogether, and substitute the word 'container'? It doesn't mean quite the same, but a bath is, among other things, a container. Using the alternative word could set you thinking along less obvious paths. Do you want to put anything besides water in the bath (coal? the laundry? the kids' rubber ducks? plants?)? Where does the water come from to fill the bath? Or you might try the word 'wash' – and consider whether you really need a bath? How about a shower? A sit-up bath? How does the bath fit in with other washing arrangements? And so on.

Unlikely associations

Another trick that takes us a little further along the same route is to consider a comparatively (at first thought) unconnected word, and see if you can work from there to your problem. Examples? Let's take the problem of supermarket stock levels, and the word 'day'. Not an obvious connection but it might make us think along the lines of, say, how often do we want to add up sales and recalculate stock requirements? Is a day a good interval? Should we do it more than daily? Could we do it continuously by electronic means? And all of a sudden, the chore of doing a weekly stocktake appears in a quite different light.

It is very easy to get stuck in a rut when you're approaching a problem. You see it one way, and even if the way you see doesn't seem to be leading anywhere, it's difficult to change your perspective. Associative techniques are intended to break the vicious circle. It's like, say, going to work. You might take the same route day after day, without ever giving it a thought. Then one day you have to visit the dentist first and you stop to think how to get from the dentist's surgery to your work. Suddenly, it strikes you that for years you have been taking a long way round. The alternative was right in front of your eyes, but you just couldn't make yourself see it.

What about that computer?

One good word to use in this associative way is staring us right in the face – it's that word computer. If you don't have a computer at the moment, you may still be finding it hard to think what exactly you would use it for. You're not a football league secretary, your kids are past the multiplication table stage, and you don't play the piano. You can't say that there have been that many occasions when you've said to yourself, 'I could just do with a computer to help me solve that problem.'

You will probably recall, if you stop to think, several occasions on which you have bought a new tool – a deep freeze, perhaps? an electric drill? – which you didn't expect to use all

73

that frequently. Yet once you had it, you found yourself using it again and again. It's as if the more you used it, the more you found you needed it, until soon you couldn't imagine how you ever did without it.

It's hardly surprising – you were using the same type of association. The new gadget was probably at the top of your mind, and when you came across a problem in your daily life (what shall I cook for supper? where shall I hang that picture?) your mind worked from the gadget to the problem, perhaps without you ever noticing.

In the future, designers, engineers, managers and house-holders will look to the computer as a versatile tool to use in the solution of a whole range of problems. We are only at the early stages of the computer revolution and, although things are changing rapidly, the use of small computers is still limited by the lack of good programs (software) as well as a lack of the right kind of sensors and activators (hardware) needed to carry out the tasks they could be asked to do.

Lastly, to reinforce some of the points we've made about problem solving in this chapter, here is our final challenge – controlling a greenhouse.

The greenhouse problem
What is the greenhouse problem? Well, we certainly know some basic facts: we know what plants are being grown and what conditions they like, how much heat or cold they can stand, how much food they need and so on. The answer: a way of controlling these various factors, when we're not around to do it ourselves. And the gap: finding that way.

Here we have to do our hard thinking in order to fill in that gap. How might we start? Well, remembering what we've said about content and context, you will doubtless realise that the problem of running the greenhouse isn't just about plants. What is it about, then? The things that make plants grow well – the temperature, humidity, light and so on, the relationship between all of these factors and the control of them.

That word 'control' is the one which might lead us to think that the computer could help us as we have seen that controlling things is one job the computer can do very well. Could it do the job in this case?

Basically, the answer is yes. The computer can't easily decide what temperature would be best, or how much food the plants need – though it could keep a handy note of these details for us, once we'd worked them out. If we told the computer what temperature and plant food we wanted, though, it could certainly

Temperature Sensor

Program

```
3.0T0337V
30  IF DAY <
40  IF TEMPERATO
750  REPEAT
3760  PROC'HEATER'
3760  UNTIL TEMPERA
3770  ENDPROC
3780  IF WINDSPEED >
3790  REPEAT
3800  PROC'VENTILATOR
3810  UNTIL OPEN= 45
3820  ENDPROC
```

Ventilator motor control

Windspeed and direction and solar energy sensors

Microcomputer

Valves controlling heat to radiators

Sensors measuring acidity and strength of liquid feed

Concentrated liquid feed pumps

How the parts of a computer-controlled greenhouse at the National Institute of Agricultural Engineering, Silsoe, Bedfordshire, link together.
Compare them with the diagram on page 36. Plants here are grown in hydroponic (soil-free) conditions using a liquid feed. The computer controls its composition.

go about keeping them within the range we selected.

What kind of input and output would be involved to enable it to do this? Sensors and actuators would be used like the ones which control that jet engine (page 10). The sensors would measure the temperature and examine soil conditions and then they would input the measurements to the processor (we look in more detail at how this is done on page 91). The processor would compare the measurements with the temperature, soil acidity and other limits it had been given, and if they didn't fit, tell the actuators to set in action the apparatus that might put the situation right – heaters, ventilators, pump, or whatever.

Just to give one example where the computer would be better at controlling, say, the temperature in the greenhouse than more traditional thermostats, consider the problem of switching the heat on around daybreak. Photosynthesis in the plants can begin as soon as the sun rises and, to get the maximum photosynthesis, the temperature needs to be raised to anticipate sunrise. During darkness the temperature needs only to be high enough to prevent freezing. The ideal controller, therefore, will know when daybreak is going to be, for every day of the year, and will switch the heat on about half an hour beforehand. This is a very trivial problem for a computer programmer to solve and it is only one of a number of things which a greenhouse control program could be asked to do to help reduce energy wastage and produce maximum yield in crops. Of course, in hot weather, keeping temperatures down is equally important, so here a ventilator control motor could be used, and linked into the rest of the system.

At this stage we would doubtless have to go back and get some more information – things like what sensors are available? what would the system cost? and at least, could we actually buy or write a program to make the computer do all this? We haven't got rid of the problem until we have our solution up and running!

In Chapter 4, we will take a look at programming one or two of the problems we've looked at in this chapter, and let you see for yourself that programming is really not such a mystery. Firstly though, we need to take a closer look at just how that computer works.

3 The hardware and the software

So far we have seen roughly what the computer is like, what sort of things it does and how it fits into the business of problem solving. Now it is time to take a look at how the computer is actually put to work. We need to take the human being with his problem, the computer with its processor, memory and so on and look at the way in which we close the gap between the two.

We've called the computer a tool for the problem solver, but we need to go a little further and look at how this very special tool differs from other tools – hammers, drills, sewing machines or the like.

The adaptable machine

With traditional technology, a machine was designed specifically with a task in mind. Take a simple machine consisting of a couple of cog wheels. The design of the cogs determines precisely what the machine will do – in this case change the direction of rotation and speed of a shaft. What goes on is completely predictable and is determined by the ironmongery – or the hardware, if you like.

If we want to alter the machine in any way – say, to change the ratio determining the change in speed between the cogs – we have to change the hardware. This means physically redesigning the system.

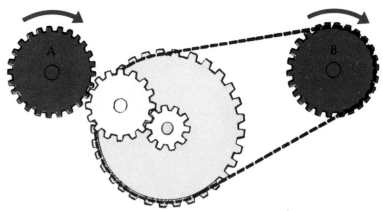

When we use computer technology, an entirely new concept is required. What happens in a computerised system is not immediately obvious because what happens is determined not so much by the hardware but by the program of instructions fed in to the computer 'black box' from the outside. To alter what the machine does we simply alter the program – or the software as it is called. It is not necessary to alter the hardware physically at all. Changing the software instructions enables the computer to do different things.

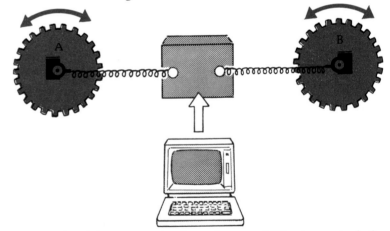

So the flexibility we gain through our ability to control the hardware by using a series of instructions is the key to computer technology. This has meant that a new breed of person has evolved to cope with these new concepts. We hear of people called 'software engineers', 'programmers' and 'systems analysts'. Most of these people work not with screwdrivers, soldering irons and other hardware tools, but with paper and pencil and the keyboard, creating instructions for the computer.

'Programmable' machines.
However versatile the computer, it would be quite wrong to think that it was the first ever programmable machine. Jacquard's loom, 1862, (top left, p 79) could weave different patterns in cloth according to programs stored on sets of punched cards (shown at the top of the machine). Inspired by the loom, piano makers developed similar devices (like the one shown extreme right, from the Musical Museum, Brentford). The paper roll, (inset), has the music punched into it. Air, sucked selectively through the holes as they pass over a perforated metal plate, operates the playing mechanism. Composers like Rachmaninov 'recorded' on pianos like this one.

Below, a computer-controlled robot builds up the opening title sequence for a recent television series.

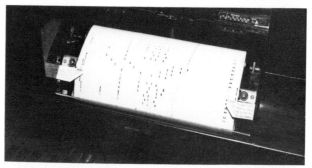

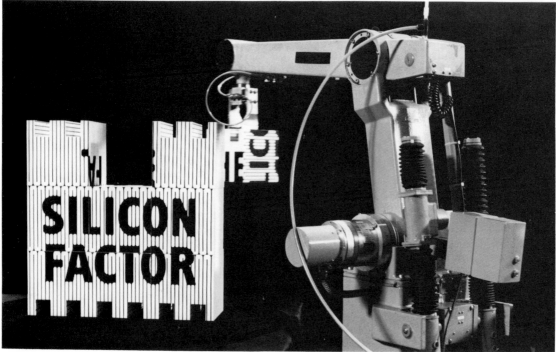

We saw in Chapter 1 that the computer's versatility is based on only a few fundamental things – adding two numbers together, subtracting them to see if one is bigger, smaller or the same as the other. On its own, of course, the computer can do nothing; we have to tell it to do tasks which involve computing and we have to use a language which it can understand. This means programming it, and usually involves using a keyboard. It is possible to program some computers in what is known as a 'high-level' language – that is, in a language which in some way resembles the language we use ourselves. At other times, it is necessary to use a 'low-level' language – for example, when the instructions are entered in the simpler but much more incomprehensible 'machine code' of 0s and 1s discussed on page 96. In this chapter we take a look at some of the things going on inside the black box when the computer operates.

Playing the game. A 'dedicated' microcomputer and its dedicated clientele. The machine has been programmed to perform only the one (admittedly complex) task.

At this point it is quite important to make a distinction between, on the one hand, 'all-purpose' computers which we, the users, can program ourselves and, on the other, machines which may well contain microcomputers which have been programmed by their manufacturer to do quite specific things. The latter are 'dedicated' microcomputers. The television-based games found in pubs are of this kind – and so are the newest washing machine controllers: with the games you might play Space Invaders or nothing; with the washing machines you may be offered a wide choice of programs – for whites, coloureds, delicate fabrics and so on. You can select the most suitable one, but if you don't like the choice you are offered, that's too bad. You can't tell the machine to wash clothes according to a program you devise – you have to stay within the manufacturer's selection. If the whites' cycle is at 70°C and has three rinses then that's that. It's just too bad if you want to wash at 65°C and with four rinses.

The kind of computer we are interested in here is the kind which can be programmed *by the user* with a series of instructions fed into its memory in a form which it can understand.

Programs and software

A program is a series of instructions. The vital word here, though, is not 'instructions', but 'series'. The point about the programming concept is that it is not necessary to give the computer one instruction, wait until it has carried it out, and then give it another instruction – instead, we give it the whole series of instructions at once. That is what the automatic washing machine's program does, too. It tells it how and when to stop one operation and go on to the next, so it can move through the various washes and rinses in a cycle without stopping for more input from the user.

The computer's program has one great feature – which some people have called the 'intelligence factor'. It is the opportunity to give the computer alternatives to carry out, depending on what it finds out as the result of carrying out previous instructions. Take, for example, the procedure of deciding if an umbrella is needed before we go for a walk. We might program a robot to decide if it needs an umbrella, by giving it five instructions:

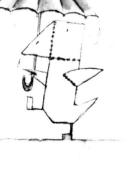

1 Open door.
2 Look at the sky.
3 Is it cloudy or raining?
4 If yes, pick up umbrella.
5 Go out.

We saw alternatives like these in the flow charts we wrote in the last chapter, and we will see more of how the computer handles them in Chapter 4. This ability to make decisions, and as a result of them to take different paths through the program, is the one thing that makes the computer unique.

The software

We have already said that the program is part of the computer's software, as opposed to its hardware. The sort of program we talked about above – and the sort we wrote flow charts for in Chapter 2 – is called an 'applications program'. It is a program fed in from outside which tells the computer how to carry out an application. However, the computer has to know how to understand the program.

If the program is written in the computer's binary code, and tells it exactly what to do at each stage, that's no problem for the computer. But for many applications it is preferable to write the program in a 'high-level' language, one which is easier for us to understand than the binary code instructions. To do this we use a program *already in the computer* to translate these instructions into the binary codes which it understands. The 'interpreter' – and this is analogous to a language interpreter – is also software.

Nearly all computers are made with some of these decoding instructions built into them. In fact, they aren't something you, the user, give the computer, nor do you need to understand them to use it – they are something the manufacturer has made a part of the machine. When the instructions come in this form, they are sometimes referred to as 'firmware'. The firmware then, usually contains everything the computer needs to know before it can run the 'applications programs' fed in from outside.

We'll return to look in more detail at some types of software later in the chapter. First, we need to take a longer look at just how the computer's hardware gets to work.

Inside the computer

A simple way of explaining how the computer works is to use a simple analogy – that of a railway system dealing with coal trucks. As all analogies have their limitations, do treat this one in the spirit in which it is offered!

Imagine that there is a main line along which trains arrive, and a main line down which they eventually depart (this is like INPUT and OUTPUT in the computer). Each train which arrives has on its front a number (an ADDRESS) which says which siding (MEMORY LOCATION) it is to go to, and has eight trucks, some containing coal, others empty (the DATA). As it arrives, each train passes a controller who operates the points to direct the train into the siding which has the same number as the number on the front of the engine. Let us imagine that two trains arrive – one is directed to siding number 20 and contains five tons of coal and the other is directed to siding number 21 and contains seven tons. The controller also receives instructions (a PRO-GRAM), say down the telephone line, and he writes these instructions on a blackboard in his hut. Both the sidings and the blackboard contain all the information he needs. His job is to sit there all day, directing the trains in and out of the sidings and into the yard where new train loads of coal are made up according to instructions he has received. Imagine his instructions read:

1 Take the contents of the train in siding number 20 and move it into the yard.
2 Take the contents of the train in siding number 21 and add it to the contents of the first train.
3 Store the result in siding number 22, until the main line is clear.
4 Send it on its way.

*One way of showing how the computer deals with numbers
(see the explanation on p. 83).*
Bottom right is the schematic diagram showing the similar relationship
between the various electronic components of the computer. Note that the
'program' and the 'rules' are both examples of 'software', and so is the data
(the coal in the trucks). The rest is hardware.

OUTPUT

INPUT

WORKING MEMORY

CENTRAL
PROCESSOR

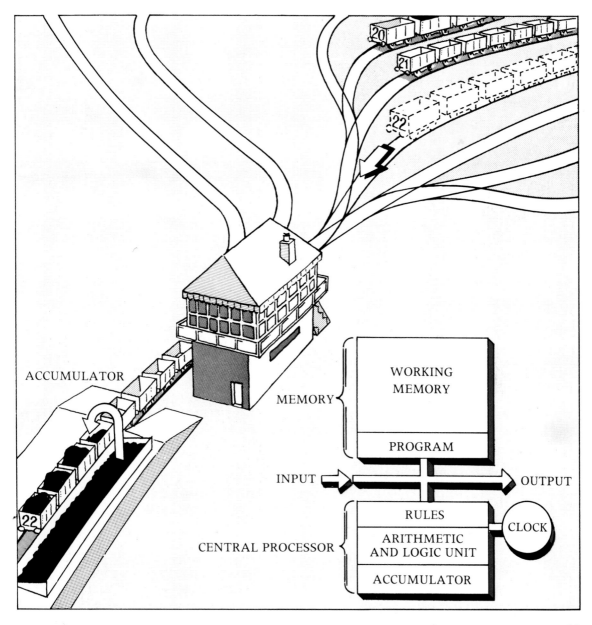

ACCUMULATOR

MEMORY

WORKING MEMORY

PROGRAM

INPUT

OUTPUT

CENTRAL PROCESSOR

RULES

ARITHMETIC AND LOGIC UNIT

ACCUMULATOR

CLOCK

The controller operates the points and knows that only one train can move at once and that there is only room for one train in the yard at once. He has his own *local* rules about this. He directs the first train into the yard (the ACCUMULATOR) and it dumps its five tons of coal there, and moves back to its siding, empty. The second train is then directed to the yard and dumps its seven tons, again returning empty. The yard now temporarily has accumulated twelve tons. An empty train arrives, fills up with the twelve tons and goes off to wait in siding number 22 until such time as the controller sends for it – to send it on to the main line (the OUTPUT). The controller is responsible for the directing of the trains, altering the points, receiving and looking at the instructions and for what goes on in the yard. His empire includes an area of the processor called the ARITHMETIC and LOGIC UNIT (ALU) and he is controlled by a clock and has his own local timetabling rules. Of course, as we have seen, the computer can add, subtract or compare two numbers, so in our imaginary railway the controller might get instructions which say 'If the contents of the train in siding 20 are the same as that of the train in siding 21, then send the train from siding 21 to Bournemouth. If not, send it back to siding 21.' A curious exercise for a railway, but necessary to complete our analogy.

Now, bearing our analogy of the railway in mind, a recap of how the computer works should be a little clearer. Most micro-computers handle numbers that are 8 bits long, and each memory location has a 16-bit number giving its address. Packets of data coming from the input in the form of 8-bit numbers are directed by the central processor to a memory location defined by an address. Each number is now taken out of the data memory in order and, according to the instruction given by the controller, is added, subtracted or compared to the result of previous manipulation. A special memory location has to be supplied to hold the previous result – this is usually within the control area, and is called the accumulator (where the results accumulate after each instruction has been completed). To make sure that the data reaches the processing area in the correct order, and at the correct time, some form of clock and local monitoring program is needed.

Hence information from the input goes to the memory location given by the address associated with it. When the program – the list of instructions – is working, data is moved from the memory, according to those instructions, and manipulated in the arithmetic logic unit, or ALU. Once the instruction has been carried out, it is put back into a memory location, or moved to the output.

In our example above, the instructions – in computerspeak – would be something like this:

1 Load the ACCUMULATOR with the contents of memory location 20
2 Add the contents of memory location 21
3 Store the result in memory location 22

In the accumulator the value of memory location 20 turns out to be 5, that in location 21 is 7 and the result is 12. So we have a very simple program for adding two numbers together.

The different kinds of memory

An 'EPROM' – A special kind of read-only-memory chip which can be programmed by the user. The program will stay there quite safely until the user wants to re-program it by first erasing it with a burst of ultra-violet light. Hence its name – Erasable Programmable Read-Only-Memory.

Read-only memory

In most computers it is useful to have some of the instructions or, in the case of dedicated computers like that in the washing machine, whole programs *permanently* stored inside the computer. There are particular kinds of chips which enable us to do this so that the memory is not lost even when the machine is switched off. These are called 'ROM' chips. ROM stands for 'read-only memory'. ROM is rather like a book of instructions – the controller can look things up in it but the contents do not change. As we mentioned above, the decoder which helps the computer to read a program is usually put into the computer by the manufacturer. We called this 'firmware'. ROM is firmware. The word 'non-volatile' is often used to describe this kind of memory – meaning that it is not destroyed when the power is switched off.

Random-access memory

The other kind of memory found inside computers is called RAM – 'random-access memory'. Another name for it is 'read/write memory'. RAM chips are the kind which lose their contents when the power is lost – so this kind of memory is sometimes also described as 'volatile'. If read-only memory is like a book of instructions, random-access or read/write memory is rather like a blackboard on which you can scribble down notes, read them and rub them out when you've finished with them. In the computer, RAM is the working memory. If the dedicated computer's program is held permanently in ROM, then on the other hand in the programmable computer the program is loaded (written) into RAM from outside.

Back-up memory
The last kind of memory which concerns us is 'back-up' memory. This is memory outside the main body of the computer in which programs can be kept for future use or in which data can be kept until the computer is ready to use it. It could be a cassette tape or a magnetic disc or drum and is needed for two reasons:

1 The computer's working memory is only of a finite size and may not be able to hold all the data it needs to use.
2 The back-up memory is 'non volatile' – it does not disappear when the power is switched off; only if it is *intentionally* erased by the user.

Three sorts of 'back-up' memory: the 'floppy-disc' – removed from its protective container, the punched paper card (now almost extinct) and the tape cassette for home use.

What about the expression 'random access'? The best way to understand this is to think of the difference between the domestic tape recorder and a gramophone record. On the tape recorder, if we want to find a piece of music in the middle of the tape we need to run through the tape to get to that part before we can play it. With a gramophone record we can lower the stylus down wherever we want and find that 'band' right away. The gramophone gives us 'random access'; the casette recorder does not. Is back-up memory 'random' access? Some is, some is not!

If a domestic tape recorder is used to store data, then a given piece of data can only be found by running through the tape to

How the 'read/write' head can move across the floppy disc to give 'random access' to its stored information.

that point. The magnetic disc, though, does give us virtually random access. The recording or playback head can go to any part of the disc very quickly and write or read information stored at that point straight away.

To summarise this, all the instructions that orchestrate the activities of the computer – like taking instructions from the keyboard, sending characters to the screen, accepting programs from casette or disc – must be kept in ROM. This type of ROM is usually called the *monitor*, as it monitors what's going on in the system. In most small computers the details on how to understand the program instructions are also kept in ROM. In some circumstances, applications programs will also be in ROM. All the instructions and data that the computer uses (or creates) in the course of running a program will be kept in RAM.

Moving between the memory and the processor

Getting information into and out of the memory is quite a complicated task. You will remember from page 37 that most common microcomputers can potentially store up to 65,536 bytes (each containing 8 bits) of information and each byte lives in a separate memory location, with its own address.

Using another analogy, consider the information to be stored as similar to the contents of a letter. The letter contains information and has to be sent from one address to another. The letter is put into an envelope and posted to the location given by the address on the envelope. When it reaches the desired location, the letter is taken from the envelope and kept at the new address until something else needs to be done with it. This is exactly how the computer handles information. Thus, whenever information has to be transferred from one memory location to another, this is done by knowing the source and destination addresses.

The bits and pieces

If you open up a computer and look inside you will see it consists of a number of silicon chips fixed into a complex web of wires on a printed circuit board. One of the bigger chips is the central processor and other chips form the memory – some of them are the read-only memory chips and others the random-access memory chips. Then there are other chips which connect with the input and output devices which form part of the computer's complete system.

Inside the BBC Microcomputer
1 The Central Processor
2 The clock
3 The random access
(working) memory
4 The read only memory
   (containing BASIC) etc.
Many other chips are needed to
perform a range of functions – such
as controlling the screen, and
communicating with the various
other 'peripherals'.

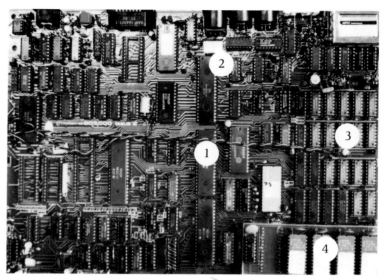

The central processor   The microprocessor is the most important component, with quite
an assortment of functions. These include:

1   Controlling all the different parts of the computer.
2   Keeping the operations in time sequence.
3   Performing arithmetic and logic operations – the job of the ALU,
    with the help of the accumulator.
4   Transmitting data and instructions to and from the input and
    output and the random-access memory.

The 'Bus'   In any computer, the controller, the clock, the ALU and accumulator, the ROM, the RAM and sufficient other circuits to enable
all these to communicate with each other and with the outside
world, are connected by a thing called a 'bus'. A bus is simply
the name given to a number of wires forming a communication
path between different parts of the computer. The bus structure
starts inside the microprocessor connecting its various parts and
is continued on the outside where it is expanded to do a lot of
other jobs. The bus in the computer is usually divided into four
sections as follows:

1   The power supply to all sections of the computer.
2   The control bus which carries all the control signals.
3   A two-way data bus which sends data and instructions to and
    from the processor and memory.
4   An address bus which sends the address of the data which is on
    the data bus.

Unlike a real letter, the address of the information moving around the computer is sent separately from the data or instructions travelling from or to that address. Separate busses are used so as not to get mixed up. It might mix *us* up, but the computer really does find it easier this way. The busses are usually constructed as a series of parallel conductors. They are clearly visible on the photograph above.

Communicating with the computer

So much for how the various bits of the computer communicate with each other. We'll now go on to look at how the computer communicates with the outside world, through its forms of input and output.

We have seen that processing information is at the heart of any computer system. It must be stressed that information will only be processed in accordance with the program put into the computer. The computer is unable to think for itself. Information presented in an unexpected way will not be dealt with properly and if the machine is asked to process information in a way that it has not been programmed for, it will blindly try to continue until it comes to a grinding halt. Information comes in many forms, and both the input and the output units must be able to 'translate' information into or from the form that the computer can handle.

Dealing with the real world

Unfortunately, not all of the information we would like to put into a computer system is easily available in the form that the computer can handle. Many computer-based systems are used for controlling *things*. Robots used on production lines to make cars are one of the more sophisticated uses. Modern cars are using microprocessor-based systems in one form or another. Cash registers, central-heating controllers, television games, watches, microwave ovens, cookers and many other consumer products now have microprocessors or small computers inside.

The information used in these appliances comes in all forms from continuously varying quantities like temperature, to simple on-off information from a light switch. The latter is obviously easy to handle – it's already in a form which the computer can deal with using the 1s and 0s of its binary arithmetic 'On' = 1, 'Off' = 0. There is no problem when the computer has to handle decimal numbers: we saw on page 34 how it translates them into its binary numbering system. The problem comes when continuously varying information – called *analogue* data – has to be converted into separate numbers, or *digital* data. (Both decimal numbers and binary numbers are forms of digital data.) Most computers can only work with digital data – and it must find a way of treating this analogue information as if it were digital. Conversely, the information coming out of the computer is digital, and this has to be converted into analogue form if a continuously varying output is required.

Typical examples of devices which provide analogue information are thermometers, pressure gauges and electrical meters using needles. As we move into a computerised world, some of the traditionally analogue means of measuring information are already being converted into a digital form. Take a digital watch, for example. A watch with second, minute and hour hands is an analogue device. It doesn't give you the time in numbers but as a continuously changing pattern in space. By contrast, a digital watch tells us the time directly in numbers.

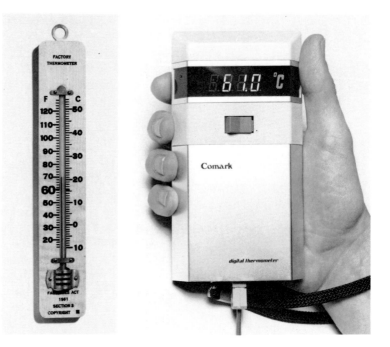

Analogue and digital.
In the analogue devices (the watch with hands and the wall thermometer), time and temperature change continuously. In the digital versions, at any instant they are given a number which can change by a minimum discrete amount (say by one second in the case of the digital watch or one tenth of a degree in that of the thermometer).

In our daily life, we don't see these two ways of presenting information as being that much different. But to a computer the difference is vital, and it must find some way of converting the analogue to the digital.

The two graphs illustrate the ideas further.

Top – To the naked eye the analogue thermometer produces a continuously increasing temperature, represented by a smooth curve.

Below: The electrical thermometer's analogue output voltage is read every minute and converted into a number (digitised) in the converter. The computer receives a stream of 1's and 0's corresponding to the number. To the computer, the temperature appears to jump up every minute and stay constant in between. [Temperatures could, of course, be sampled more frequently]

Analogue to digital conversion involves measuring the value of the analogue quantity – e.g. temperature – at regular intervals – and converting the measurement into a number of pulses corresponding to that measurement. For example, assume that the temperature of an oven increases by 10°C every minute, as in the graphs below. If the temperature was measured every minute a series of numbers would be produced – 10, 20, 30, 40, 50, 60 – each one corresponding to the temperature at that time. This, basically, is how the computer handles analogue data. A converter measures the variations (e.g. of the voltage from an electronic thermometer) at regular intervals, say once a minute or a thousand times a second, and presents the measured data to the computer. If the computer knows the time between each measurement, it can build up a digital version of what's going on.

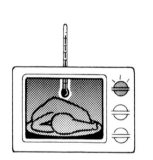

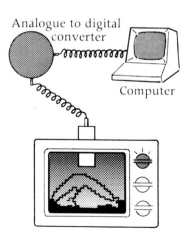

Analogue to digital converter

Computer

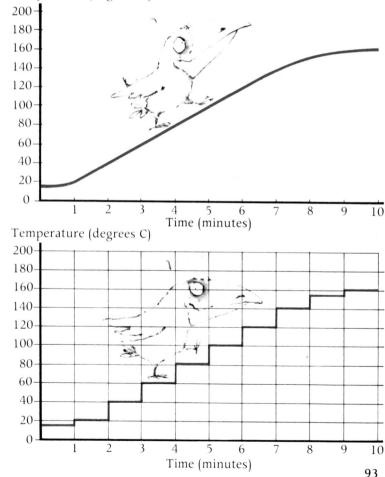

These are very simplified examples of what really happens. But they do illustrate the fact – a very important fact – that the computer can not only handle information presented in the 'accepted' way, but also *any* form of information as long as there is a way of converting it into digital form. This means that even complicated forms of information – sound waves, for example – can be analysed by a computer. Similarly the *output* from the computer can be in practically any form required.

Another example of conversion

To explore this business of converting information into and out of the computer's binary digital form further, look at the way the computer uses an ordinary cassette tape (the kind you buy with music recorded on it) to store its binary digital information. Basically, the information stored in the computer's internal memory is read out fairly slowly and put onto the tape. This cannot be done directly as tapes respond to sounds within the

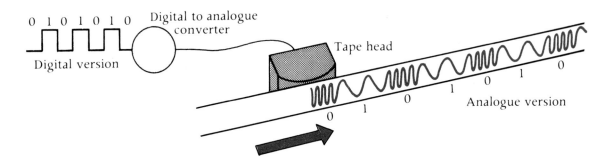

Digital to analogue conversion when a program is stored on a magnetic cassette tape. The '0's' and '1's' are recorded as analogue tones of different frequencies.

frequency spectrum that we can hear – that's what cassette recorders have been designed to do. The data has first to be modified, and one of the easiest ways is to represent a 0 by one frequency tone and a 1 by another. When the cassette is played back through the computer interface, the reverse process happens.

This business of analogue and digital conversion may seem complicated but for the computer it is a great deal easier to go through this process and obtain objective information from something like a thermometer than it is to go through the infinitely more difficult process of understanding human beings and their language! Much of the rest of this book is about just that: the way the computer succeeds (and, in some directions, still fails) in understanding its human masters and what they want from it. In this chapter, we'll tackle this problem by looking at the half-way house of computer languages. In Chapter 6, we will look at the business of voice input and output. But for a start a comparatively easy operation for the computer: printing a single character in the form we like to see it.

The computer makes a letter 'D'

Of course, there is a very simple way of making a letter 'D'. You make a pre-formed letter, like the 'D' in a typewriter, and you tell the computer's printer to produce an impression of it through a form of impact printing. That works fine, except you need a separate piece of metal or plastic for each letter and character you want to put on paper. After a while a practical machine starts to run out of characters. It will generally manage to provide all the characters on a standard keyboard in one typeface, but what if you want to produce Arabic or Chinese characters, or do graphic illustration?

One kind of printer popular with microcomputer owners works in a different but more versatile way. It consists of a row of pins – or in some cases just one pin – which strike the paper to produce dots. A processor in the printer sends a stream of 1s and 0s, and each makes the printer print a dot or miss one out. Printers like this print seven dots – or, in the better machines nine – close together in a vertical row. They will then move the print head along a dot's width and print another selection or all of the seven dots. By doing this several times they build up a letter; by doing it a whole lot of times they can print a line of text.

The dot matrix printer at work. The pins strike the ink ribbon and thus make an impression on the paper. Then the print head moves on a fraction and the process is repeated.

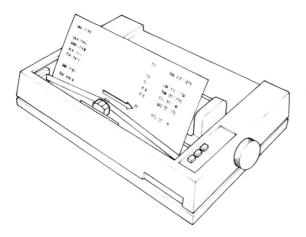

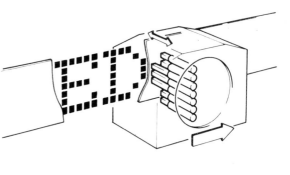

On receiving a completely different pattern of 1s and 0s, the same print head can print all kinds of fancy characters – including Arabic and Chinese.

Programming languages

Just as there are many human languages, so there are many computer languages. These have developed in a similar way to human language. For example, the earliest men probably had a limited vocabulary and were therefore able to communicate limited concepts. As man developed so did his language; as he became more sophisticated so more abstract concepts could be discussed. Similarly, when children are learning to talk they use a few words to describe everything – as they learn more, and their needs become more complicated, so their language becomes more sophisticated.

The same thing has happened to computer languages. In the early days, people programmed using the computer's binary code, or what we call 'machine language'. When this became difficult, mnemonics were used to make life easier. This is called 'assembly-language' programming. Finally, there are the 'high-level' languages like BASIC, FORTRAN and ALGOL. These are much more similar to everyday language, and are translated directly or indirectly into the computer's machine code using the computer's firmware. BASIC is the language most often used to introduce programming, which we will look at in some detail in Chapter 4. Few microcomputer owners will be interested in actually programming in the low-level languages, but for the sake of completeness, here is an idea of what it involves.

Machine language

This is the language which the computer actually understands deep down inside itself. When we use a higher-level language the computer itself translates our instructions into machine language. Some computers can be programmed directly in machine code. It is tedious and time consuming as you can see from the following simple program of 1s and 0s:

```
10100101        00100000
01100101        00100001
10000101        00100010
```

This is the series of instructions which make the computer actually add two numbers together, and is written in the machine code of a popular microprocessor. It is clear that more complicated tasks would be very difficult to program. One way of simplifying it is to replace each group of four binary digits with a rather more compact code called 'hexadecimal'.

Hexadecimals The word hexadecimal refers to a counting system based not on 10s or even 2s but 16s. There are 16 numbers that can be defined by four 1s and 0s – starting with 0000 and finishing at 1111. The table below gives them all, together with the decimal equivalent and the hexadecimal code.

Decimal	Binary	Hexadecimal
0	0000	0
1	0001	1
2	0010	2
3	0011	3
4	0100	4
5	0101	5
6	0110	6
7	0111	7
8	1000	8
9	1001	9
10	1010	A
11	1011	B
12	1100	C
13	1101	D
14	1110	E
15	1111	F

You'll notice that we ran out of digits for the hexadecimal column. As we were working in 'base 16', instead of 'base 2' for the binary and 'base 10' for the decimal numbers, six other symbols were needed. The letters A to F are used.

Hexadecimal numbers can be used in the same way as binary ones, and easily replace them. For example the 8-bit binary number 1010 1110 can be written as the hexadecimal number AE. Each group of four binary numbers is represented by one hexadecimal number, and vice versa. Converting between the two is easy with the aid of a table. (Doing the same between decimal and hexadecimal is far more difficult.)

If we look at our example of machine code and replace the eight digit groups by their hexadecimal equivalents we would then get the following:

A5	20
65	21
85	22

A hexadecimal keyboard on a computer which can only be programmed in machine code. Pushing 'E' produces the code 1110, the equivalent of the number 14.

This is easier to read, but just as difficult to understand! If the codes on the left are replaced with mnemonics representing the hexadecimal instructions, the program now becomes:

```
LDA        20
ADC        21
STA        22
```

Or in English:

Load the Accumulator with the contents of address 20
Add the contents of address 21 to the number in the accumulator
Store the answer in memory location 22 (which should ring a bell – see page 87).
The programmer has to know the first number he wants to use is in memory address 20, the second in 21 and answer in 22.

Assembly language

Going one stage further we could call the two numbers ONE and TWO. We could also call the program ADD. It would now look like this:

```
ADD     LDA    ONE
        ADC    TWO
        STA    RESULT
```

As long as the computer knows where the program started in the memory – identified by the label ADD – and what memory locations have been allocated to ONE, TWO and RESULT then the program should work. This is obviously a very simple example and in practice things are more complicated. A whole range of translation programs have been written, and these are called 'assemblers'. These convert the assembly language program into the binary machine code and thus the assembly language codes can be typed in at an ordinary keyboard.

High level languages

There are a whole host of high-level languages, and most have been written for one particular type of application or another. For example, ALGOL has been written for general applications, COBOL for business applications, FORTRAN for mathematics work and BASIC for general-purpose introductory programming.

The latter is the easiest to use on small computer systems, and is consequently the most popular. Unfortunately there are many different forms – or dialects – in many of these languages. Which one your particular computer understands depends upon the software which it uses to translate the BASIC program into its binary code. This makes things difficult if programs written for one computer system are tried out on another. They will be incompatible and will need translating.

Which language should you use?

A high-level language like BASIC is more efficient in programming time, and is much simpler to use than assembler. Other programmers can also understand what has been written, which is useful if you want to exchange programs. Assembly language and machine code, on the other hand, give the programmer the ability to use the computer to its fullest capacity.

In general, BASIC is most suitable for 'interactive' applications where the operator and computer want to 'talk' to each other. Simple calculations, games, and other general-purpose programs – such as training programs – are easier at this level.

Assembly language, on the other hand, is more suitable for the control of peripherals and input/output routines, and programs *within* the computer system. It also makes maximum use of the small memory capacity of microcomputers.

High-level languages are usually the easiest method for the majority of personal computer owners to use. Programming in a high-level language such as BASIC is considerably quicker than in assembly language. Machine coding is very time-consuming to write, but machine-code programs usually run faster than programs written in high-level languages.

Putting words inside the computer

We've said that the computer handles characters – letters and numbers, as well as signs like *, / and so on – quite as much as it does arithmetic. We've only talked about binary, though, as if the computer is getting ready to do arithmetic. Stop for a moment to see how the computer puts characters into a code of binary 1s and 0s. Remember, arithmetic in binary isn't really a code: it's just a different number base for counting than the 10 we use most of the time. When we put characters into binary it really is used as a code.

Since we use the same 8-bit (1 byte) binary characters to stand for both numbers and characters, we have to tell the computer which we are storing. To avoid taking up part of the code, this is generally done in the address of the location in which we store the byte. In that one byte of information, we can easily find codes for each character on the standard QWERTY keyboard (very easily, you might say, reflecting that there seem to be nearly 10 times too many).

The 'QWERTY' keyboard.
Each key can produce one of two codes: one when the shift key is untouched – giving, say, '1', ';' and '9' – and one when it is held down – giving 'L' and '+' and ')'.

Do we really need so many? Well, there are 26 upper case letters and 26 lower case (remember, a computer is a very stupid thing: 'A' is quite different to 'a'). There are 10 numbers (0 to 9) and 35 odd characters like '', ', &, £, etc. The machine also needs characters for 'invisible' symbols like 'space' and 'end-of-line'. In one way and another, there isn't a lot of change out of 128 characters – which is just how many you can represent using 7 bits ($2^7 = 128$).

Aha! says the alert reader: 'I thought we were talking about 8 bits' ($2^8 = 256$). This is perfectly true. The reason for the disparity is that one bit is saved up to cope with possible mistakes caused by sending these characters down noisy, crackly telephone lines. The eighth bit can be set to 0 if there are an even number of 1s in the character; to 1 if there are not. In this way the computer at the other end of the line can check to see whether there's been a garble. If there has, it can ask for a repeat. This eighth bit is called the 'parity' bit.

We won't explain exactly what codes the computer uses for which characters, but it is worth mentioning that these codes, when looked on as binary numbers, correspond to the alphabetic order of the characters that are being encoded. A is 'smaller' than B, and so on. This allows whole words to be 'counted' and compared with others. This technique is used when sorting words into alphabetical order, or pulling all those starting with X, for example, from a list, or in the telephone directory program in Chapter 1.

The limits to the hardware?

One of the most important things about the microelectronic technology which lies behind today's generation of computers is its smallness. The electronics is 'micro', the computers are 'micro', everything is 'micro'; and they are all getting even smaller. Already people in Japan are talking about putting the power of an IBM 370 – a computer that fills a large room – onto a single chip a quarter of an inch square. What's the point? you may be wondering. Do we really need a powerful computer that's so small it could get lost in your pocket? Would not a microcomputer be just as useful – or useless – if its processor were six inches or a foot square instead of a quarter of an inch?

The reason why smallness matters is buried deep in economics and physics. To see why, we first have to take a look at what a chip is and how it is made.

A close look at chips

A chip, say a microprocessor, is simply a very great many electronic switches which control each other in various ways. You could make a device which did the same things rather slowly if you had the money, patience and space, out of old-fashioned post-office relays. Each switch on a chip is a microscopically small transistor, similar to the transistors in a radio but on a minute scale. Transistors are solid-state devices: that is, they have no moving parts. They are made of a material that acts as a semiconductor – that is to say a substance which can allow electricity to flow under some conditions but not under others. Most chips today are made of silicon, and areas of the silicon are 'doped' with impurities to turn them into semi-conductive devices. When the chips are operating, only minute amounts of currents are used, which enables the transistors to be crammed very close together without overheating.

The usefulness of a processor or a memory made up of some tens of thousands of these transistors depends on two things:

1   How many there are.
2   How fast they work.

The speed of operation depends on two things:

1   The actual operating speed of a transistor, the time it takes to switch from on to off, or vice versa.
2   The time it takes to send the resulting signal to the next transistor.

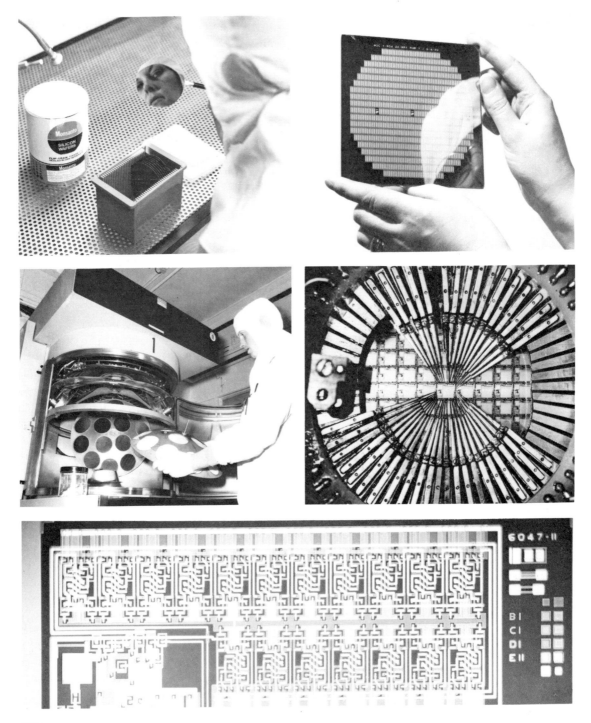

Stages in the Manufacture of silicon chips.
Top left: A wafer of pure, polished silicon is inspected in dust-free conditions. Next it will be heated to form an oxide coating and covered with a photosensitive emulsion.
Top right: A 'photographic mask'. This contains a repeating pattern of minute lines which are exposed onto the silicon. Where the light falls, the emulsion changes and can be dissolved away, leaving an exposed area which can be chemically treated in various ways: etched away, coated with another substance or impregnated with a 'dopant'.
Centre left: The treated disks of silicon are exposed to a 'dopant' – like the element Boron – in this ionising chamber. The dopant changes the electrical properties of the silicon.
Centre right: Testing the chips. Each rectangle is a chip – one of hundreds on the surface of the treated wafer. Minute, precisely aligned needle-like probes make contact with the connecting points and all the circuits on the chip are put through their paces. The chips that 'pass' are separated and then packaged up (see page 39).
Bottom: The surface of the chip, showing the way that these processes produce layer after layer of change to make up the final integrated circuit. The top layer consists of metal connecting wires which are 'condensed' on to the surface.

The smaller the transistor is, the quicker it works; and the shorter and narrower the connecting lines between transistors, the quicker they work.

The process of putting the various devices onto silicon is done rather like printing on paper – we'll come to it in more detail below. However, for the moment what matters is this: just as a printing works can only print a certain number of acres of paper a day – a number that is determined mainly by the initial investment in machinery – so a silicon chip factory can only produce a certain area of silicon a day – an area limited by the amount of expensive equipment it has. It turns out that the cost of a chip is mainly proportional to its area, and has very little to do with how complicated it is. In other words, it is just as expensive to produce a 6-in diameter wafer of silicon carrying a single transistor as it is to put 400 devices on it, each consisting of 100,000 transistors. (American chip makers talk about the area of silicon they can process as the 'Real Estate'.)

We can now see the reason why smallness is important in microelectronics. Since it doesn't make much difference to the final cost how many transistors go on a chip, the more there are the cheaper each one is – or you can offer more computing power at the same price. If that were the only advantage, it would be well worth going for smaller devices.

However, there are other advantages too – as the transistors get smaller, and the lines thinner, the chips become proportionally even more powerful. A new device, with lines half as wide as an old one, other things being equal, can have eight times as many components at the same cost.

Of course, there is a limit to how small we can make the devices. Apart from the difficulty of drawing the lines, the components of the chip behave differently when built at a very minute scale. We can, however, expect to keep on making more tightly packed, more powerful chips until they reach roughly 200,000 times the power of today's. Since device densities have roughly doubled each year since 1960, at that rate we might expect the pocket computer to have the processing power of a quarter of a million of today's microcomputers by 1990.

The smaller the devices, the more problems there are in making perfect chips, and the higher the reject rate. Rough calculations suggest that halving the line width (increasing the power of the device by a factor of eight) reduces the yield of usable chips from 30% to 1%. To overcome this chip makers may have to do some lateral thinking, and try an entirely new method of mapping the pattern of devices onto the chip.

At the moment chips are made using a photolithographic process. As the lines get narrower, however, visible light becomes an unreliable medium; its wavelength is too long, and the lines get fuzzy at the edges. The next step will be to use X-rays, which have a smaller wavelength, or electron beams.

Future hardware and software

There is still a lot of mileage in miniaturisation. When the practical problems get too great, the hardware engineers have a lot more extraordinary ideas up their sleeves – everything from using light particles instead of electrons, to cooling the whole computer down to near absolute zero. But is more computing power really what we need?

In time, we can expect to find the power of large mainframe computers on a single chip. Big libraries will be written into read-only memory, so that a piece of equipment the size of a calculator may well contain the complete *Encyclopaedia Brittanica*, or its equivalent.

However, as we sketched at the start of this chapter, the problem is not so much compressing information-storage and increasing computing power; it's knowing how to use the computing power when you've got it, which is the role of the software provider. Many computer people believe that developments in software, in learning how to put to use the extraordinarily powerful machines we already possess, will be far more important than further developments in hardware over the next 10 or 20 years, in other words, thinking of ingenious new ways to program the computer. There is every chance that the next 20 years of computing may be even more interesting and surprising than the last 20 years.

At this point we've reached a position where we're ready to look at just what *we* can program the computer to do, and how *we* go about it.

4 Understanding programming

We have already talked a little about what programming is and what computer program languages are. In this chapter we're going to take one particular language, BASIC, and look at how it is used – at what is involved in writing some simple programs. First, though, a word about the language we've chosen.

BASIC

BASIC means 'Beginner's All-purpose Symbolic Instruction Code'. It was originally developed at Dartmouth College in the USA as a high-level language that would be easy to learn and to teach. It was mainly intended for people who knew nothing about computers but were keen on using them. Since then BASIC has been further developed and become extremely widespread throughout the world. Hundreds of thousands of different computer programs have been written in BASIC, many of them available in books and magazines. Its recent rapid increase in popularity has stemmed from the speed with which it can be learnt and from its ready availability on microcomputers. Most microcomputers, and many larger computers, have software which enables BASIC programs to be run on them.

In some people's eyes, BASIC is not the world's best programming language but it is one of the most approachable – especially for beginners, as its full name implies – and that is one reason why it has been chosen as the main language for the BBC

Computer Literacy Project. One of BASIC's virtues is that the various commands lead on very simply from ordinary written language. What follows is an indication of how the language can be used: it is not intended as a course in how to write BASIC programs – another part of the BBC Project does that.

However, if you can struggle through and follow this chapter you stand a good chance of being able to write programs yourself, and then there is no substitute for trying it out on a computer of your own, in your own time and at your own pace.

There are many different sorts of programs you can write in BASIC but even if it isn't the best language for every program – just as any one microcomputer won't be the best for every conceivable application – it is a flexible language. You may find you would like to learn other languages later, but you will get quite a fair way on BASIC alone – even if using it is sometimes like getting a Frenchman to understand your English!

There's BASIC, and BASIC, and . . .

One of the problems with BASIC is that, rather like English, it is a language which can be spoken in many dialects. Different dialects in computer languages use different words and symbols to mean the same thing; sometimes, too, they let us do different things. Sadly, unlike in English, where someone from Yorkshire can understand someone who comes from Somerset, computers working in BASIC will only 'run' if the appropriate dialect is used. Luckily, at the simplest end of the language most of the instructions and rules are common to most dialects, so what follows should apply to many microcomputers on the market.

We must stress, though, that we are trying to illustrate what programming is about, not to teach you all about it. If you have a computer and want to set about some serious programming you will need much more detailed information on what your particular computer can do, and which dialect it understands. As a general illustration, you should find this chapter helpful but for a detailed guide you will need to refer to the instructions that accompany your machine or to do a course on programming like the one associated with the BBC project.

Some of the attractive things which computers can produce in the way of graphics output or sound can also be controlled using BASIC. However here the various instructions involved are most likely to be unique to the particular machine you are using. Because these and other more sophisticated instructions are 'machine specific' – to use the jargon – we will not deal with them here.

The fundamentals

Some things are common to all languages, including BASIC. They all have some way of dealing with the four fundamental activities on which nearly all programs are based:

1. Getting things into and out of the computer.
2. Comparing things.
3. Deciding if something is true or not, and, if so, doing one thing or, if not, doing another.
4. Doing something a number of times until some condition is met.

These are the basic abilities the language has. What differs from one language to another is the way it sets about doing them.

Earlier on we looked at the three things the processor can do in a computer: add, subtract and compare numbers. When a program in a high-level language – like BASIC – is running, every part of the program is translated automatically by software inside the machine into simple steps which involve the processor doing just those three things and it's possible to use a language like BASIC without knowing anything about what happens inside the 'black box'.

You will remember that the computer can only deal with one instruction at a time, and that it needs to know in what order to deal with the instructions in a program. Virtually every dialect of BASIC uses one simple and very useful tool to help it do this: *it numbers every line in the program.*

Line numbers

In the programs we write you will see that each instruction, or group of instructions, has a number. The computer starts at the lowest number in the program and works its way through. It doesn't necessarily carry out the instructions in strict numerical order, though. Instead, it can be told to jump from one to another. In fact, computer programs written in BASIC tend to look like a game of snakes and ladders. Simple programs just start at the beginning and go through to the end but most useful programs are not like that! Instead, 'ladder' instructions tell the controller to shift upwards to a later line number and 'snake' instructions slide it back down again.

Incidentally, line numbers in BASIC are usually written going up in 10s. The reason for this is a very practical one – if we want to insert extra lines at a later date, it's then possible to do so. We'll see all this later when we come to look at ways of making programs easier to understand.

The ins and outs

Everything we 'tell' the computer we have to 'input' into it; and everything the computer tells us it has to 'output' to us. Of course, there are different ways of getting information into and out of a computer, but we'll assume we are putting information in by typing it in at a keyboard, and the computer is giving up its replies on a screen. Two practical things to note:

1 When the computer is switched on it will display a 'prompt' – some word or symbol on the screen which shows when it is ready and waiting for a command. We will ignore prompts in most of what follows.
2 Every micro has a button labelled ENTER or NEWLINE or RETURN. This is produced whenever a 'packet' of information typed at the keyboard has to be 'posted' to the computer. Again, on the whole we will not indicate the points at which this button needs to be pressed.

The first thing we have to do, then, in getting the computer to do something is to give it instructions (unless they are already inside the computer, of course). Let's say we want our computer to add 3 to 4. We would type in an instruction. What would that look like? Well, it would look pretty much like:

$3 + 4$

We've forgotten a couple of things, though. Most important, we don't have any way of finding out what the answer is! In fact, we'd never just tell the computer to add $3 + 4$. We would always tell it to do something with the answer. Do what? It might:

1 output it to us
2 store it somewhere for use at a different point
3 use it immediately for some operation.

If we type PRINT $3 + 4$ and push the RETURN or ENTER button then the computer answers immediately: 7.

What does PRINT tell the computer to do? It doesn't tell the computer to add 3 to 4: the $+$ sign does that. What it does is to tell it to *output* the result. It is one of the peculiarities of this language that we use PRINT when we mean output, even if it's not printed output we want but words on a screen.

Suppose we want it to do something more complex. We can join together a whole series of instructions like PRINT $3 + 4$ with line numbers in front to show the order in which they are to be done.

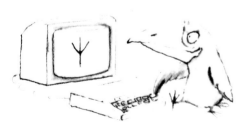

PRINT

10 PRINT 3 + 4
20 PRINT 5 + 6

A sequence like this is a *program* and it is not executed immediately – it's stored. The individual instructions in the program are
called *statements* and, naturally, the numbers in front are the *line
numbers*. To execute the program you have to type the *command*
RUN. What RUN does is to transfer the control of the computer
from the operator (you) to the stored program. The computer is
no longer waiting for you to tell it what to do; it follows the
instructions in its stored program.

RUN will tell the computer to go to the lowest numbered
line in the program (line 10, in this case), and work through
until it reaches the end. Then it'll display READY, to show it's
ready to do something else. (*Note:* in some dialects the program
should always end with a statement END or STOP.)

When an instruction like RUN is entered by the operator
without a line number, to be carried out immediately, it's called
a *command*. When it's part of a program it's called a *statement*.
So in BASIC, PRINT, for example, can be used as a command or
as a statement – depending on whether it's the operator (you) or
the program that's in control at the time.

So, we have two operations in our short program: PRINT and
+. We don't include the RUN command in the program itself,
though we need it to make the program work. All the keywords
like PRINT that the computer recognises we will write in capital
letters, to distinguish them from other words we use in the
program and because many computers expect keywords to be
typed as capital letters anyway.

When we RUN our program, then, what will the computer
output? Try it yourself, if you have a computer to use. What
you should see on the screen is:

READY
RUN
7
11
READY

A SEQUENCE OF
STORED INSTRUCTIONS

A COMMAND

109

Filling out the dialogue

That's fine as far as it goes, but it doesn't go very far, does it? 7 *what*? we might be thinking to ourselves. Perhaps it would be better if the computer output read:

$$3 + 4 = 7$$
$$5 + 6 = 11$$

Let's modify our program. We would have to write this:

10 PRINT "3 + 4 ="; 3 + 4
20 PRINT "5 + 6 ="; 5 + 6

Running *this* program will produce just that result. But how?

Numbers and characters

You'll have realised that the vital difference between the first 3 + 4 and the second 3 + 4 is the inverted commas " ". To make this clear, we have to draw a distinction between numbers and characters. What's the difference? Take, say, '123'. As characters, that's a 1, a 2 and a 3. As a number, it's a hundred and twenty-three. Anything between inverted commas is called a '*string*' and the computer regards it as just a sequence or string of characters without any special meaning.

Letters are characters too, and the inverted commas mean that the computer will keep whatever's between them, numbers or letters, exactly as it is. Instruction keywords between the inverted commas will also be treated as characters, so the computer won't take that first + as an instruction to add anything together.

We can use this convention to make the computer print just about anything. Then, by using punctuation marks like the semicolon and the comma between print statements we can display the words on the screen in different ways. Here are some examples: on the left are the programs, on the right the results of running them:

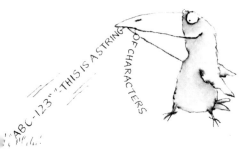

	The programs	The results
1	10 PRINT "BBC, LONDON"	BBC, LONDON
2	10 PRINT "BBC," 20 PRINT "LONDON"	BBC, LONDON

3	10 PRINT "BBC, "; 20 PRINT "LONDON"	BBC, LONDON
4	10 PRINT "BBC", "LONDON"	BBC LONDON
5	10 PRINT "BBC, "; "LONDON"	BBC, LONDON

You will see that punctuation marks between inverted commas are ignored as instructions; they are merely part of a string of characters. So in example 1 above, the comma after BBC is not significant as an *instruction* to the computer. The same is true in example 2, only here there are two PRINT statements and the computer prints them on separate lines. Example 3 has a semi-colon after the inverted commas. This instructs the computer to print the next thing on the screen right up against the first. So, punctuation marks *outside* pairs of quotation marks are able to be instructions to the computer; those inside are not.

Example 4 uses a comma instead of a semicolon. This tells the computer to separate the print statements by about a quarter of the width of the screen. (It's like the tabulator on a typewriter.)

Example 5 produces the same result as example 1 but has two print statements separated by a semicolon. The semicolon, as we have seen, prints one right against the other. Notice that to avoid the result BBC,LONDON a space has to be included here before LONDON in the second statement, or after BBC, in the first. These rules may appear a little strange at first but you should soon find them becoming clear when you see how they are applied.

Replying

It would be a move forward if we could get the computer to say hello to us personally. Of course, we could do that by putting our name into the computer program. But we can also do it by putting our name as data for the program to use, as it's running.

You will remember in Chapter 2 how we distinguished between instructions and data, and we said that (broadly speaking, and with some exceptions which we will come to later) the data is put into the program while it is running. So far we've been talking about putting the program itself into the computer. Now let's think about putting the data to the program.

We use another instruction to tell the computer to obtain some 'input', and this time it's just what you would expect:

INPUT. It tells the computer to do two things: to wait for some input at that point in the program, and to display ? on the screen – so we know we've got to input something.

Just as the computer has to do something with that answer, so it has to do something with the input: find somewhere to put it. And before we see how the INPUT statement works, we must look at the business of 'locating input'.

Variables

As we said earlier, one very important job the program language and the associated software have to do between them is to find a place to put all the information when it is not actually being processed.

In BASIC, we don't have to identify a storage location where the information will be put. In other words, we don't have to tell the computer, 'Slots 34789 to 34850 in the memory are empty: put this word in there.' But we do have to tell the program to make room somewhere to store the information, and we do this by setting up 'a variable'. A variable is the name we give to the location. The idea of the variable is one of the most important in computing. Mathematicians will find no difficulty with it, but others might. To help, here is another analogy. One way of thinking of a location is to think of it like a box or a pigeon hole with a name on it. The name tells you what the name of the box is but not what is inside it. What goes inside the box can be changed but the name of the box cannot. In the computer program, the box with its name is the variable. The variables can have different values in just the way that the box can have different things inside it, but it can only have one value at a time.

In a BASIC program there can be two kinds of variable – two kinds of 'box'. One is called a 'numeric variable' and it can only have a value represented by a number. The name of the variable must begin with a single letter, followed if necessary by a number or the rest of a word. In some versions of BASIC only the first two letters of the word will be significant (this means that if we were to call one variable 'age' we should not call another variable anything beginning with 'ag').

The other kind of variable is called a 'string variable'. A string variable, unlike a numeric variable, can be anything we like: a 'string' of *characters* – whether they are letters or numbers or both. Providing we enclose them in quotes, numbers and symbols will be treated as characters by the computer. It won't change them, and can't do any arithmetic on them. The contents

Worms = 4

of string variables must *always* be put in inverted commas and to let the computer know what kind of variable we want, all string variables must end with a dollar sign $. Below are some examples which should help to make this vital but confusing state of affairs clearer.

Numeric variables

Name
Can be one or more letters or a word, eg A or AGE or a letter followed by a number, eg a2
Value
Can only be a number, eg 85 or 85.23

String variables

Name
Must end in $
Could be a word, eg name$, or a letter, eg N$ or letter + number, eg n2$
Value
Anything in quote marks, eg "Father Christmas", "Father Christmas, age 85", "85 years"

If we now go back to our input command and tell the computer to input our name, we need to make available a string variable, since names are not numbers. We can then use commands we have already met to make the computer say hello to us.

10 PRINT "WHAT IS YOUR NAME"
20 INPUT name$
30 PRINT "HELLO, "; name$

And some notes of explanation:

Line 10
When we use the INPUT statement, all that is going to appear on the screen is a question mark. If we want to know what we have to input, we have to tell the computer to ask us. That is what this line is doing.
Line 20
You will see that we don't have to tell the computer to set aside

a location called name$. When we first use the location name name$, the computer will automatically do this. All we have to tell the computer to do is wait for the input, and then it will allocate it to the variable name$.

Line 30

Look carefully at where the inverted commas come. We don't want inverted commas round the variable name$. If we did have them, what do you think the computer would print? Right – not the contents of the 'box' but its name, ie not Peter (or whatever your name is) but name$. The semicolon tells the computer to print the words next to one another. So it's important to leave the space after HELLO,.

We've now reached the point at which we can hold a conversation with the computer even though we have to tell the computer in advance what to say! If we take that last programme again, and underline our side of the conversation we could see this on the screen:

```
RUN
WHAT IS YOUR NAME
?
JANE
HELLO, JANE
READY
```

That takes us quite a long way but before we go on to the next stage, actually solving a problem on the computer, we must take a look at the most important aspect of programming: telling the computer to make decisions.

Decisions and branches

Let's take a new problem as our example for this section: checking passwords.

If you have ever used one of the new cash dispensers which are appearing in the walls of some high street banks you will know that it is necessary to enter a personal code as well as your cash card before you can withdraw cash. If you fail to give the right code after a few attempts, you may lose your card, while if your reply is right, you can go ahead with the withdrawal. Many computer systems use a security system of passwords or passnumbers before individuals can gain access.

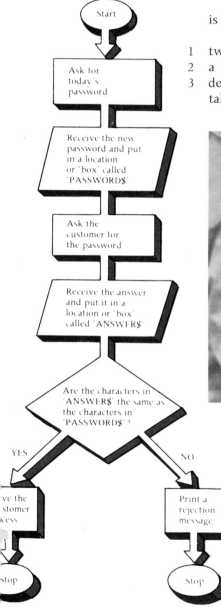

We can draw a flow chart to show how such a system could work. This particular system might be used, for instance, at the beginning of a bigger computer program, to enable you to allow only those customers who know the password to use the program. What is more, you (the programmer) could change the password as often as you want.

Most systems give the customers several attempts, but that is a refinement we'll leave till later. You'll see that we have:

1 two points at which data is put in,
2 a point at which the two pieces of data are compared and a
3 decision point at which the computer has a choice of routes to take.

Flow chart boxes:

- Start
- Ask for today's password
- Receive the new password and put in a location or 'box' called 'PASSWORD$'
- Ask the customer for the password
- Receive the answer and put it in a location or 'box' called 'ANSWER$'
- Are the characters in 'ANSWER$' the same as the characters in 'PASSWORD$'?
- YES — Give the customer access — Stop
- NO — Print a rejection message — Stop

How do we program this? Let's give the program first, and explain the new features afterwards:

```
10 PRINT "PROVIDE TODAY'S PASSWORD"
20 INPUT password$
30 CLS
40 PRINT "PLEASE GIVE PASSWORD"
50 INPUT answer$
60 IF password$ = answer$ THEN GOTO 90
70 PRINT "HELP! CALL THE POLICE!"
80 STOP
90 PRINT "CORRECT. YOU MAY PROCEED"
```

Lines 10 and 20 you should be able to follow. Line 30 contains a new instruction present in some dialects of BASIC – CLS – which clears the screen, in this case for obvious reasons. But what happens in line 60? We have three new key words: IF, THEN and GOTO, as well as another instruction – the symbol = These all mean just what they say. If whatever follows the IF command is true, then we are given special instructions. If it is false, these instructions don't apply, and we carry on to the next line of the program. These special instructions tell us to 'jump' and *go to* line 90. So in this case, we wouldn't carry out the instructions on the lines between here and line 90 at all.

Note: In some better BASICS it is possible to rewrite this program more simply using an ELSE instruction:

```
60: IF password$ = answer$ THEN PRINT "CORRECT. YOU
    MAY PROCEED" ELSE PRINT "HELP! CALL THE POLICE".
```

IF MOUTH OPEN THEN FEED
— ELSE DON'T

In fact, lines 70 and 80 form the right-hand branch of our program and line 90 is the left-hand branch. We must put STOP or END at Line 80 otherwise HELP! CALL THE POLICE would immediately be followed by CORRECT. YOU MAY PROCEED. There are only two choices: either the data in the two locations is the same, or it isn't. We could, however, have several IF . . . THEN statements in a row if there are more than two possibilities. We'll see this in later programs.

We must always put some other statement after the IF statement, so that we know what the special instructions are. This will usually be either a THEN or a GOTO or both, as we put in our program above. In some dialects, we don't really need the THEN in line 60, because the GOTO tells us what

Goto bed!

to do. Some dialects demand THEN every time, so we'll leave it in. Some insist on GO TO and will not run if the space is left out, instead telling you there's an 'error'!

Note: If a computer doesn't like something you've written into the program it may do one of a number of things:

1 Print SYNTAX ERROR or MISTAKE when you try to run the program.
2 Print a longer error 'message', giving details of where the error is – for example, what line it is in.
3 Refuse to let you enter the line in to your program at all until you have found the error.
4 Print an error number (which you need to look up).

Looping the loop

One of the other fundamental things we can ask a computer to do is to repeat something a fixed number of times or until some condition is met. For example, we could modify our password program to give the customer three chances at the password before sounding the alarm.

This time we'll put the line numbers from the new program against the relevant boxes in the flow diagram on the next page.

```
 10 PRINT "PROVIDE TODAY'S PASSWORD"
 20 INPUT password$
 30 CLS
 40 LET mistakes = 0
 50 PRINT "PLEASE GIVE PASSWORD"
 60 INPUT answer$
 70 IF password$ = answer$ THEN GOTO 120
 80 LET mistakes = mistakes + 1
 90 IF mistakes<3 THEN GOTO 50
100 PRINT "HELP! CALL THE POLICE!"
110 STOP
120 PRINT "CORRECT. YOU MAY PROCEED"
130 END
```

We've only introduced one new keyword, LET, but we've done quite a few new things:

Line 40
LET, used like this, is the way we name a new variable. We are,

117

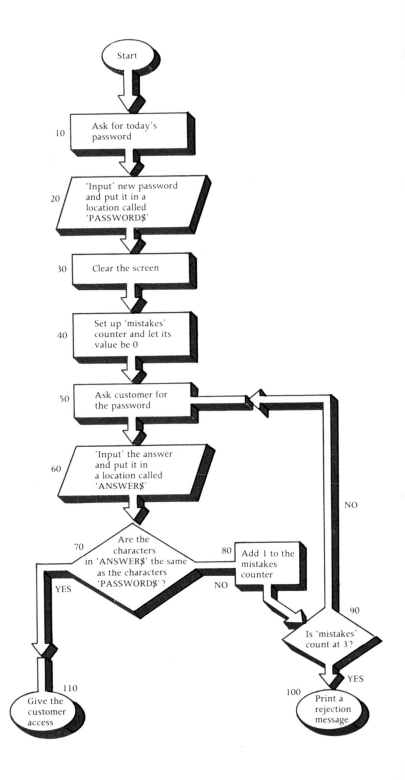

Start

10 Ask for today's password

20 'Input' new password and put it in a location called 'PASSWORD$'

30 Clear the screen

40 Set up 'mistakes' counter and let its value be 0

50 Ask customer for the password

60 'Input' the answer and put it in a location called 'ANSWER$'

70 Are the characters in 'ANSWER$' the same as the characters 'PASSWORD$'?

80 Add 1 to the mistakes counter

YES

NO

NO

90 Is 'mistakes' count at 3?

YES

110 Give the customer access

100 Print a rejection message

WORMS = worms + 1

as it were, naming a 'box' which we are going to use later to count the number of wrong guesses. And this is a numeric variable, so its name, mistakes, doesn't have a $ sign. Initially there have been no guesses, so the value of mistakes is set at 0.

Line 70

This time, we do have two . . . IF statements running, because there are three possibilities: the customer is right, he's wrong but has another chance, or he has been wrong three times.

Line 80

This is how we change the value of a variable using the LET instruction. (The new value in the 'box' is the old value plus 1.) This often causes confusion because mistakes = mistakes + 1 looks like a maths equation that doesn't balance. It isn't like that. It means, effectively, let the new value be equal to the old score plus one!

Line 90

Here we introduce another condition and if it is met, the program returns to line 50. The condition asks if the number in the mistakes 'box' is less than 3. If it is, then the customer can have another go. If it is equal to 3 then the condition is not met and the program goes on to line 100. The ⟨ sign means 'less than'.

Note: If ⟨ means 'less than', in a similar context ⟩ would mean 'greater than', = would mean 'equal to' and ⟨ ⟩ would mean 'not equal to' – in other words 'either less than or greater than'.

If you have a computer, try out these programs, putting in different right and wrong answers. If you don't, you can still try them out by imagining how the computer would work down the program if you put in various answers.

Documentation

We've gone quite a fair way towards having the computer tell us what it's doing and what input it wants. What we haven't yet done is to provide a full explanation of what each part of the program does in the program itself.

You may feel we don't need to in these short programs but if you have stored a number of programs on the same cassette, say, or if you have written a very long and complicated program, it is a great help to provide a little more explanation. We call these explanations 'documentation' and we use a new keyword, REM (for 'Remark') to put them into the program.

The computer doesn't do anything whatsoever with what we write inside a REM statement. It just skips over it when the program is running. Nor does it print out the remarks. To find out what they are, we have to use yet another command, LIST.

Typing in LIST will make the computer list the program in its memory. To be a bit more selective, we can type, say,

LIST 50

and the computer will just display line 50. Or

LIST 50, 80

and it will show lines 50, 80 and all the lines in between. This command is useful to alter a line which contains a mistake.

We'll tie all this together by going back to one of the problems we used in Chapter 2, the test on the times table, and seeing how we might set about programming that.

A child's maths test

You'll remember that in Chapter 2 we drew up a very simple flow chart for this, and added a more complicated one for doing the test by hand. Now we'll draw up one for doing it on the computer, and add two extra features. We'll have the computer talk to the child by name, and we'll limit the number of wrong answers the computer will accept on any single question to four.

```
  1 REM Program to test multiplication
  2 REM by asking random questions
  3 REM using numbers between 1 and 12
 10 PRINT "What is your name"
 20 INPUT name$
 30 PRINT "Hello, "; name$;" – Let's try this question"
 35 REM Generate two random numbers
 40 LET a = RND(12)
 50 LET b = RND(12)
 55 REM Set counter for errors to zero
 60 LET count = 0
 70 PRINT "What is "; a ; "x"; b
 80 INPUT answer
 90 IF answer = a*b THEN GOTO 170
100 LET count = count + 1
110 PRINT "Wrong."
```

115 REM Check if there have been four errors
120 IF count = 4 THEN GOTO 150
125 REM Offer another try if count is less than 4
130 PRINT "Try again. You've had "; count; " tries."
140 GOTO 70
150 PRINT "You've had four tries. The answer is "; a*b
160 GOTO 180
165 REM Advise if answer is correct
170 PRINT "Well done, " name$
175 REM Offer additional question
180 PRINT "Want another go"
190 INPUT reply$
200 IF reply$ = "YES" OR reply$ = "Yes" OR reply$ = "yes"
    OR reply$ = "y" OR reply$ = "Y" THEN GOTO 40
210 PRINT "That's all!"

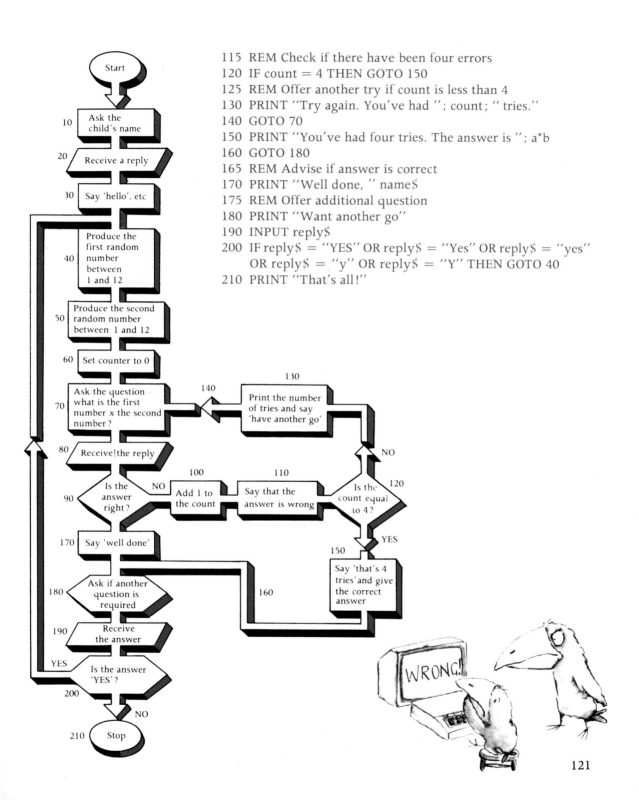

$$a = RND(6)$$

Lines 40 and 50 are designed to generate random whole numbers between 1 and 12. It's like throwing dice, electronically. We will not attempt to explain how this is done but the random number generator is a useful technique. (*Note:* In some BASICs you will need to type in something more complex to get this to happen.) In line 90, the symbol * means 'multiply' to the computer. In line 70 we wrote x, but as it was enclosed in quotation marks the computer does not treat it as an instruction but as a string character. In line 200, the computer has just asked the child if he or she wants another go. The child might type in YES, yes, Y or Yes and the computer asks itself if any one of these has been entered. The computer will only recognise the reply if it is exactly in the form it has been told to look for. Because the computer is incapable of guessing your intention, any sort of reply other than these (e.g. 'all right', 'if you like') will send the computer to line 210. Note the way the new keyword 'OR' is used.

There are many conversations we could have with the computer if we ran this program, depending on what our replies were. Take one 'run' of the program. Our replies are indicated.

```
READY
RUN
What is your name
?
George
Hello, George – let's try this question
WHAT IS 5 × 6
?
35
Wrong
Try again. You've had 1 goes
25
Wrong
Try again. You've had 2 goes
30
Well done, George
Want another go
?
NO
That's all
READY
```

It's hardly an Oscar winning dialogue but it's a real conversation and every response the computer makes shows us it has taken notice of the last thing we said to it.

We could improve this program in many ways. We could ask which table the child wanted to answer questions on and ask a set number of questions (perhaps checking to make sure we didn't repeat any). We could keep a running total of the number of right and wrong answers, and tell the child at the end of the test, with a suitable comment ('That's very good, George', 'Not bad, George', 'Sorry, you failed' or whatever you fancy). What other improvements can you think of? With the programming tools you've already acquired, you should be able to think of ways to try to program quite a few of them for yourself.

'Bugs'

You may have noticed that there is a small flaw in the program, and there may be others. In 'computerspeak' mistakes in logic or in the actual coding of the program are called 'bugs'. Often these may go undetected for some while because the program works perfectly well, most of the time.

The flaw here is a trivial one. When in line 130 the program says PRINT "Try again. You've had "; count; " tries" this is fine when the count of the number of tries is two or three. But if it is the first try, the program will produce Wrong. You've had 1 tries which is ungrammatical to us but not to the computer. This could easily be dealt with; can you think how?

There is a vital point to be made here: it is very difficult to check programs for every conceivable eventuality. The larger the program the more difficult it is and many programs being sold (or published in magazines) contain bugs. Some of these may be programming errors – an obscure IF-THEN branch, for example, might lead to a computer syntax error if one condition is met but the program might run perfectly well otherwise.

One simple example might be a program which invites a response Y or N in answer to the question 'Do you want another go?'. Suppose the person running the program types in 'You must be joking'. The computer may well treat the first Y as 'Yes' and act accordingly.

Three more techniques

The next program is a 'jargon generator' – an amusing way of producing high-sounding phrases like 'viable on-going situation', to add a touch of bogus class to memos or correspondence. We won't give you a flow chart for this example, but we had better explain what we will be doing in the program.

We are going to take three different lists of 'jargon' words, with 24 words in each. The first two lists will contain adjectives, and the third nouns. Then we will set these up in three lists in the computer. Next we will pick random words from each set to make up jargon phrases using one word from each list. (For this we will use the random number generator we used in the times table example.)

The program introduces three new ideas:

1 *Putting data into the program itself*
So far, we've talked as if all the data we need for our program is going to be put in while the program is running. Often, though, you'll have all the data for your problem available when you are writing the program. If there is quite a lot of it, you will find it more convenient to put the data into the program itself.

This situation is the big exception to the general rule we outlined in Chapter 2, that the program is a set of instructions, and the data is what the instructions are carried out on. In this instance, the program contains the data too!

Two new keywords are used: DATA, which tells the computer that what follows is just that – a list of bits of data – and READ, which allocates the data into whatever variable 'boxes' we choose to name. Data and read commands are particularly useful when we want to enter lists of things into the program.

2 *Arrays*
In computing, an *array* is the name given to what we might call a list. It is a list of variables, each place in the list being like a separate 'box'. As before, the variables can be numeric or string variables. Imagine a postman delivering letters to a row of box-like houses in the same street. Each house has a different number. The letters will have the same street name but different numbers for the different locations.

Similarly we might call our array in the computer A$(10), meaning we had ten 'boxes' in the 'list' called A$ and each of the boxes could have different contents. (*Note:* Sometimes the number of boxes could be eleven because the first box can have the name A$(0), just to add to the difficulty!)

In the following program we are going to make room for our three lists of words by creating three arrays. We need to tell the computer to *make room* for the arrays and to do that we use a DIM statement (DIM for dimension). In other words we tell the computer that we want it to make space available of a particular dimension for some data. We then 'read' the data into the boxes one at a time using our third new idea as given below.

3 *The 'for-next' loop*

This is a second useful way of looping the loop (see page 117) and is possibly the most difficult idea to grasp but it is the last one we'll be introducing!

Described in words the FOR-NEXT loop goes something like this: For every value of a variable from 1 to, say, 24 do something and then alter the value of the variable by one. Go on doing whatever it is until the value of the variable is 24, then stop. In the case of our lists of data we are saying to our 'postman':

1 Here is a list of data with 24 items.
2 For every value of *n* from 1 to 24.
3 Read the *n*th bit of data and put it in the appropriate *n*th box in the row of boxes called A$. For example, put the 5th bit of data into the 'box' named A$(5).
4 Then increase the value of *n* by 1. In other words go to the next value of *n* which in this case is 6 and then take the 6th bit of data and put it in the box named A$(6) and so on.

In our 'jargon generator' program this procedure is used for each of the three lists of words to get them in the computer. We then have a procedure for picking one of the words from each list at random and then printing the three one after the other to produce the jargon phrase. Here's the program:

```
 5 REM JARGON PHRASE GENERATOR
10 REM RESERVE SPACE FOR ARRAYS
20 DIM a$(24)
30 DIM b$(24)
40 DIM c$(24)
50 DATA basic,divergent,programmed,operational,affective
51 DATA child-centred,multi-,emotive,disadvantaged,on-going
52 DATA informal,ultra,interdisciplinary,cognitive,relevant
53 DATA correlated,extra-,innovatory,viable,supportive,elitist
54 DATA micro-,creative,advanced
60 REM FILL FIRST ARRAY WITH DATA
```

FOR CHICKS = 1 TO 6
 GIVE WORM.
 NEXT CHICK

```
 70  FOR x = 1 TO 24
 80  READ a$(x)
 90  NEXT x
100  DATA meaningful,procedural,significant,democratic
101  DATA sociometric,consultative,empirical,unstructured
102  DATA implicit,perceptual,psycholinguistic,coeducational
103  DATA reactionary,motivational,academic,conceptual
104  DATA socioeconomic,hypothetical,ideological,theoretical
105  DATA developmental,compensatory,diagnostic,experimental
110  REM FILL SECOND ARRAY WITH DATA
102  FOR y = 1 TO 24
130  READ b$(y)
140  NEXT y
150  DATA situation,over-involvement,evaluation,components
151  DATA disfunction,methodology,quotients,re-organisation
152  DATA rationalisation,activities,communication,resources
153  DATA synthesis,validation,techniques,consensus
154  DATA maladjustment,sector,criteria,autonomy,analysis
155  DATA polarisation,objectivity,strategy
160  REM FILL THIRD ARRAY WITH DATA
170  FOR z = 1 TO 24
180  READ c$(z)
190  NEXT z
195  REM GENERATE 12 JARGON PHRASES
200  FOR m = 1 TO 12
205  REM CHOOSE 3 RANDOM NUMBERS
210  LET a = RND(24)
220  LET b = RND(24)
230  LET c = RND(24)
235  REM PRINT RANDOMLY SELECTED WORDS FROM
     ARRAYS
240  PRINT a$(a);"   ";b$(b);"   ";c$(c)
250  NEXT m
360  END
```

FILLING AN ARRAY

Lines 20/30/40

Here we are naming our three arrays. Since they will contain
characters, we have to add the $ sign. The DIM (for DIMension)
statement tells the computer that these are arrays, and how much
space to reserve for each. Each array here will consist of 24 locations. We are effectively naming the variables, too. The first
variable we use will be a$(1) through to the last variable which
will be c$(24).

Lines 50/54

We tell the computer when one piece of data stops and the next starts by putting in the commas. Our DATA statement, of course, tells the computer that everything that follows it is data.

Line 70

This starts another little loop. We are going to repeat it 24 times.

Line 80

A READ statement usually follows a DATA statement. It tells us where to put the data. And the a$ tells us we want this data to go into array a$. The READ statement tells the computer to start with the first piece of data, and to run down the list of data in sequence, unless we put in some other instruction. So we are 'posting' a piece of data into each 'box' in the array (24 times – 24, because that's what we made x on line 70).

Line 200

Now all our data is placed, we start yet another loop to use it. This one we will carry out 12 times.

Lines 210/220/230

These are instructions telling the computer to pick a word at random from each array. We are calling these random locations a, b and c. So a will be a location in array a$, b in array b$, and so on (a, b and c are random whole numbers up to 24).

All clear? Let's see what we might come up with when we run the program.

READY
RUN

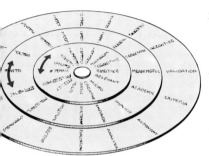

The mechanical equivalent of the computer's jargon generator. (The idea first appeared in the 'Times Educational Supplement'). Three concentric, cardboard discs can independently be spun round. As they stop the words on each disc come to rest in a random way, producing the jargon phrases.

correlated developmental communication
emotive diagnostic evaluation
advanced democratic objectivity
creative democratic disfunction
emotive implicit rationalisation
correlated empirical re-organisation
multi-socioeconomic rationalisation
ultra procedural techniques
on-going unstructured resources
emotive diagnostic components
extra-psycholinguistic autonomy
programmed meaningful maladjustment

READY

We have now introduced most of the basic rules and conventions of BASIC. Many of the concepts are difficult to grasp at first but become clearer as they are put into practice. Courses on BASIC introduce the concepts in a much more leisurely way than we have been able to do and reinforce the understanding of each one with many exercises and examples. We will finish with one last example.

Choosing a route

You may have realised that we could use this kind of approach, but with numbers as well as characters, to solve the 'route-finding' problem we looked at in Chapter 2. We'll close this chapter by seeing how we might approach it by following the solution we outlined in the flow chart on page 62.

The flow diagram and the program which follows may appear to offer an absurdly complex way of deciding how to get from A to B when there are only seven different routes. However, it should be seen as the core of a program which could be enlarged in various ways to deal with many different places and many different routes. At the various points in the program where data (details of fares, length of each journey and so on) is introduced it would be possible to introduce more data than we have at present and, provided that we altered the size of the arrays accordingly, this would enable the program to perform a very large number of comparisons and become really useful. Thinking laterally for a moment, it would also be possible to use this kind of program for other purposes – for deciding on the choice of a hotel, for example. The variables could be the type of room (double, single, with or without bath), price, the star rating of the hotel and so on.

This time we will break the program up with a description of what we are doing. In a properly documented program some of these descriptions would be condensed down into brief 'REM' statements which would be part of the program. (However, it should be noted that REM statements do use up a lot of memory space in a program.)

First, we reserve space (dimension) for our lists (arrays) of things which vary. These variables are the length of time for each journey, the method of travel (bus, train, etc.), the fare and the preferred way of travelling. There are seven different routes so we will need to set aside seven empty 'boxes' in each array by using the DIM statement.

```
10  DIM time(7)
20  DIM fare(7)
30  DIM method$(7)
40  DIM preference(7)
```

The data which needs to be put into these arrays is as follows:

Route number (R)	Time (hrs)	Fare (£)	Method	Preference
1	1.50	8.00	Train	2
2	2.20	7.50	Bus + train	3
3	2.30	6.50	Bus + train	3
4	3.00	5.00	Bus	4
5	1.00	10.40	Plane	1
6	2.50	6.00	Bus	4
7	2.30	5.50	Bus	4

We now need to fill the empty arrays with data. To do this we use the 'data' and 'read' instructions and use a 'for-next' loop *seven times* to fill up each array.

```
 50  DATA 1.5,2.2,2.3,3.0,1.0,2.5,2.3
 60  FOR R =  1 TO 7
 70  READ time(R)
 80  NEXT R
 90  DATA 8.0,7.5,6.5,5.0,10.4,6.0,5.5
100  FOR R = 1 TO 7
110  READ fare(R)
120  NEXT R
130  DATA train , bus + train , bus + train,bus , plane
131  DATA bus , bus
140  FOR R = 1 TO 7
150  READ method$(R)
160  NEXT R
170  DATA 2,3,3,4,1,4,4
180  FOR R = 1 TO 7
190  READ preference(R)
200  NEXT R
```

(*Note:* the method array is a string array and in some machines it is necessary, unfortunately, to put inverted commas round each piece of data.)

Next, we have a rather curious looking couple of lines. Later on, when the program begins to run, we might want to compare fares one at a time to see which route has the lowest fare value of the fares looked at so far. This lowest value is then held in a variable called lowest. But what happens when the first route is looked at? The program requires it to be compared with something. In this program we set the value of the variable to an arbitrary value higher than anything likely to be found in the routes to follow. It could be any value we like, and the person who wrote this program has chosen to make the value 9999. As the first fare goes through, it is compared with 9999 and found to be lower, so it becomes the new value of lowest.

The same argument applies to a variable called optimum.

```
210 LET lowest = 9999
220 LET optimum = 9999
```

We need to ask whether the customer is most concerned about the cost of the journey or the time it will take. The answer to the question should either be COST or TIME. If it is 'Cost' then the program branches one way, if it is 'Time' it branches another. But just in case some other answer has been given to the question the program asks the question again.

```
300 PRINT "What are you concerned about –"
310 PRINT "COST or TIME";
320 INPUT choice $
330 IF choice$ = "COST" THEN GOTO 350
340 IF choice$ = "TIME" THEN GOTO 350
345 GOTO 320
350 PRINT "What is the " ; choice $;" limit";
360 INPUT limit
370 IF choice$ = "COST" THEN GOTO 500
```

Lines 350 and 360 next ask the customer what limit he wants to set for cost or time. This value is then held in the variable limit. Next, depending on whether or not the choice earlier was cost or time, the program branches. Line 370 decides which way to go. If the condition is met, then the program goes to line 500; if not, it carries on. It will carry on to the next line if the choice was 'TIME'. Note the semi colon at the end of line 310 to make the '?' which is produced by the INPUT statement in line 320 print up against the end of the question produced by lines 300 and 310. It also means that the answer to the question is entered on the same line as well.

The next section of the program is used if the choice was 'TIME'. It asks for every route 'is the time for this route larger or smaller than the limit the customer has chosen?' If it is smaller then the route qualifies for more consideration and the search is on for the cheapest route which meets this requirement.

```
400  FOR R = 1 to 7
410  IF time(R)>limit THEN GOTO 480
420  IF fare(R)>lowest THEN GOTO 480
430  IF fare(R)<lowest THEN GOTO 450
440  IF preference(R)>optimum THEN GOTO 480
450  LET lowest = fare(R)
460  LET best = R
470  optimum = preference(R)
480  NEXT R
490  GOTO 600
```

best = R

In this section lines 400 and 480 establish the FOR-NEXT loop, the value of R being the route number – from 1 to 7. Line 410 asks if the time for a given route is greater than the limit set by the customer. If it is, it sends the program down to line 480 which says 'next route, please'. Line 420 asks if the fare is greater than the lowest found so far. If it is, then the route is rejected and the next route is look at.

In line 430 if the fare is less than the lowest then the program goes to line 450 and the fare for this route becomes the new value of the variable 'lowest', the 'best' route takes the value of R for this route, and the 'optimum' way of travelling is the preference for this route: 1 for plane, 2 for train and so on.

Finally we come to line 440. The program only reaches line 440 if the fare is neither greater than nor less than the lowest value found so far (in other words it is the same). We agreed in Chapter Two that if two routes cost the same amount then the decision about which one is the better depends on the preference about transport. In this instance, the program asks if the 'preference' for this particular route is higher in value (i.e. less desirable) than the preference for the previously found best route. If it is, the route is rejected. If it is lower, then this route becomes the 'best' so far. When all the routes have been looked at the program goes to line 490 and this directs it to line 600, which we'll move to in a minute.

If, earlier, the choice in line 370 had been 'COST' the program would have ignored lines 400 to 490 and gone to line 500. This section of the program does exactly what the previous section did only comparing first the cost of each route with the limit and then looking for the quickest route amongst those which qualify.

```
500  FOR R = 1 TO 7
510  IF fare(R)>limit THEN GOTO 580
520  IF time(R)>lowest THEN GOTO 580
530  IF time(R)<lowest THEN GOTO 550
540  IF preference(R)>optimum THEN GOTO 580
550  LET lowest = time(R)
560  LET best = R
570  optimum = preference(R)
580  NEXT R
```

The last section of the program looks at the results of all these comparisons and prints out the best route. If no route has met the fundamental requirement that it is cheaper than the limit or longer than the limit set earlier in line 360 then the 'lowest' value will still be that arbitrary 9999 and the program prints out 'Think again, nothing fits'. Otherwise, if all is well it takes the value of the variable best (i.e. the best route number), the value of method$ which has the value of the best route number and the values of the time and fare for this best route.

```
600  IF lowest<9999 THEN GOTO 630
610  PRINT "Think again – nothing fits"
620  GOTO 300
630  PRINT "You should travel by route"; best
640  PRINT "using"; method$(best)
650  PRINT "It will take ";time(best);" hours and"
660  PRINT "cost ";fare(best);" pounds"
670  END
```
Here is a sample 'run' of the program:

```
RUN
What are you concerned about –
COST or TIME? COST
What is the cost limit? 6.5
You should travel by route 3
using bus + train
It will take 2.3 hours and
cost 6.5 pounds
```

This program is by no means the last word on the subject! It could, for example, be modified relatively easily to print out the

route itself – in other words to say 'you should travel from London to Godminster via Camford'. The point is, of course, to give you some idea of how such a program could work, not to produce the most elegant program imaginable.

By now you should have some idea of the kind of logic involved in writing a program in BASIC. Even if you do not feel capable yet of writing programs of the complexity of the ones we have just seen, you can get a good deal of pleasure from attempting simple programs. As in any language, practice makes perfect: you could take a course in BASIC such as the one associated with the BBC project. The alternative to writing your own programs is to buy programs written by other people and run them on your own microcomputer.

The next chapter is about the practical business of having and using your own machine.

A Japanese travel agent.
Although most Japanese offices are 'paper driven', the computer is rapidly taking over. Here they can plan railway routes for you and book hotel rooms in an instant using the new technology.

5 You and your microcomputer

Why have over 100,000 people in the UK already bought their own computers when systems still cost from £50 upwards? Some of the users have a technical background but there are many more who had no knowledge of computers when they started. These include doctors, lawyers, postmen, housewives, teachers, restaurant owners, pharmacists – people from all walks of life, in fact, and their numbers are increasing all the time.

Some have quite specific applications ready for the computer – often in connection with their jobs. A growing number of people are discovering that the microcomputer offers them a fascinating new interest – an intellectual challenge which is quite addictive.

Schools are now obtaining micros and are finding that they can be used not just in the science and maths departments, but in English, geography, history, and even languages as well. Armies of schoolchildren now occupy their spare time writing programs and some countries are introducing computing into the curriculum for all children and students as an essential part of their education.

Then there are those people who feel they 'ought' to know something about computers, who perhaps feel insecure in their jobs as new technology looms over the horizon and who want the security which comes with understanding.

Others who've taken the plunge include the hobby enthusiast who prefers to put his or her own computer together – partly because it's cheaper that way, but also for the pleasure of doing the whole job alone from a computer kit.

The programmable microcomputer can be a useful tool in a wide variety of areas but it is by no means yet the miraculous device which some people would claim. It's no good buying a £100 machine and expecting it to control your greenhouse or to keep all your household records in its memory or to be able to process and print out your letters. You can do a lot with a simple system and get a lot of fun out of it. However, for the professional

```
240 INPUT answer
250 PRINT:PRINT:PRINT
260 IF answer = A$B THEN GOTO 350
270 LET count = count + 1
280 PRINT"WRONG"
290 IF count = 4 THEN GOTO 330
300 IF count = 1 THEN Z$ = "GO" ELSE
Z$ = "GOES"
310 PRINT"TRY AGAIN, "name$". YOU'VE
HAD ";count;" ";Z$
320 GOTO 230
330 PRINT"YOU'VE HAD 4 TRIES. THE
ANSWER IS ";A$B
340 GOTO 360
350 PRINT"WELL DONE":score = score + 1
360 NEXT go
370 PRINT"YOUR SCORE IS";score;" OUT
OF  ";(go  )
380 PRINT"WOULD YOU LIKE ANOTHER GO";
390 INPUT reply$
400 IF reply$ = "YES" OR ▮
```

The BBC microcomputer in its simplest form, using a domestic television set as a display and an ordinary cassette tape recorder to record programs and to play them back.

person with his eye on the future who wants to use the computer in his work, the writer who wants to build up a text processing system, the architect who wants to rationalise the calculations for tenders, the businessman who wants a cheap accounting system, it is important that the computer should be able to do a good job, and the cheapest hardware may not be enough. There is also the question of software – the computer may be physically capable of doing a job but there may not yet be a suitable program available which will enable it to do it.

Before we look at some of the many things which low-cost microcomputers are being used for, let us look at what the simplest systems can do and how some of them can be expanded.

135

The simplest personal microcomputers

So many advertisements for microcomputers are appearing in the press that the beginner, who has an interest but not much knowledge, may be forgiven for feeling bewildered. Although to some extent when you buy a micro you get what you pay for, the value of what you buy may depend in the long run more on what software is or will be available and on the extent to which the machine can be expanded than on the basic equipment you get for your money.

Well, what do you get for your money? Imagine you've just bought a typical small microcomputer. What will using it involve?

The box containing the system most likely contains:

1 A user guide, which should contain details of how to get the machine going and how to write simple programs. It will also be a reference book providing details of the use of the various instructions in the language – which will probably be BASIC.
2 The machine itself, which will have a keyboard and various plugs and sockets at the back or underneath.
3 A connection to the mains power supply which provides the low voltage on which the computer runs, either through a transformer which is inside the computer or in a separate box outside. The separate power supply is less convenient and involves yet another item to plug in.
4 A lead to connect the computer to the aerial socket of the television set.
5 A lead to connect the computer to a domestic cassette recorder.
6 There may be a sound cassette tape supplied with the equipment containing some sample programs.

Connecting the simplest system together. The leads shown
a) Connect the microphone, earphone and 'remote' (cassette motor control) sockets on the cassette player to the cassette 'interface' socket at the back of the microcomputer.
b) Connect the UHF output socket at the back of the microcomputer to the aerial socket at the back of the domestic television set.

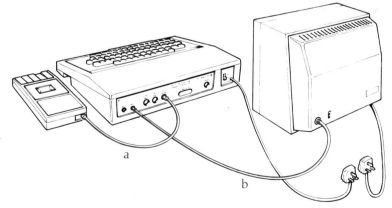

Switching on and getting going

When the computer has been supplied with power and is connected to the television set through the normal aerial socket, the first thing that needs to be done is to tune the set for the computer. A microcomputer designed to work through a television set has within it a small transmitter which produces a signal which needs to be tuned in just like tuning in to BBC-1 or ITV. Most televisions have a spare tuning knob which can be used for this and once the set has been tuned in to the computer's frequency the tuning can be left ready for next time, without interfering with the present tuning of the set for ordinary television. The computer should produce some message on the television screen – like 'READY' or a symbol like 〉 and then it's a matter of fine tuning to get the clearest lettering.

The difference between lettering on a not very well adjusted colour television screen and that on a black and white monitor. The latter gives a high resolution and can be used for up to 80 characters to the line, which is required for word processing.

Lettering on the television screen will not be quite as clear as the lettering produced by a *video monitor*. A video monitor is the kind of screen used in closed circuit television systems and does not have to be tuned to a television frequency in the way that a television set does. A serious computer user will probably use a monitor rather than a television, but it will only be possible to use such a screen if the computer has a *video* output socket. Equally, some more expensive computer systems come with their own monitors and they may not be able to run on ordinary television receivers. Black and white video monitors are fairly cheap but colour monitors are still relatively expensive compared with the domestic colour television set.

The keyboard

If you are familiar with the keyboard of a typewriter the computer keyboard should not be much of a surprise. It will have extra keys, though, and a typical layout is shown below.

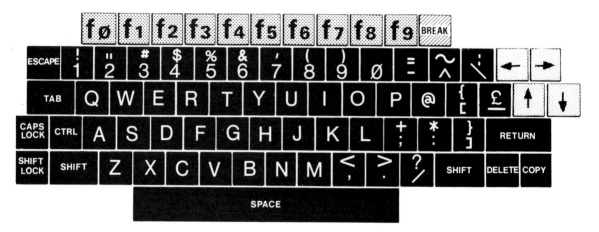

The keyboard of the BBC microcomputer, showing the (almost) standard typewriter layout, and the various specialised keys. Some of these are described in the text. The top row of keys are 'user definable'; those on the right with large arrows are the 'cursor control' keys.

The most important extra keys are:

1 The RETURN or ENTER key which is used to enter a program line or a command after it has been typed and has appeared on the screen.

2 The CURSOR CONTROL keys – these are used to move the cursor around the screen. The cursor is the marker which shows the position on the screen where the next character you type in will appear. If you want to edit a line in a computer program it will be necessary to move the cursor around to the points where the changes need to be made.

3 The BREAK key – this interrupts a program while it is running and enables you to run it again or continue programming.

4 The DELETE key – this enables you to rub out the character you have just typed on the screen if you have made a mistake.

Other keys on the keyboard have functions which are explained in the user guide which comes with the machine. Some of them may be 'user definable' keys, meaning that the user of the machine can decide (by typing in the right instructions) what each key should do. Supposing, for example, that you are writing a program which uses the PRINT statement very frequently. You may want to save yourself the trouble of always having to type in the word PRINT, in which case a user definable key can be allocated to print the word for you.

Writing and running a program

Writing a simple program is now only a matter of carefully typing in the line numbers and the statements using the rules of the dialect of the language your machine understands. At the end of each line of program, press the RETURN button, and then type in the next line.

When you have written a program type in RUN and press RETURN and the program should run. If you have made a mistake the program will stop and an error message or error number will appear on the screen. The error messages will either be self explanatory or else you will need to look each one up in the user guide to find what it means.

Most computer manuals will have programs listed in them which you can type in directly yourself. The important thing here is to type them in *accurately*. Even a misplaced 'space' could cause the program not to run.

Saving your programs – the cassette recorder

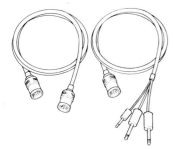

Two kinds of connector.
Left: With two 'DIN' plugs.
Right: With a 'DIN' plug and three 'jack' plugs.

Once you have slaved for hours over the keyboard composing a program which actually runs – or typing one in from the manual or from elsewhere – remember that simply by accidentally switching off the computer you could lose the whole thing – the memory will be erased and all that effort wasted. This is where the simplest kind of backing storage comes in useful. The domestic cassette recorder can be used to store and replay all the programs you type in to the computer.

Most machines will come with a lead to connect the computer to the recorder. (Make sure you have the right kinds of connector. The two most popular are shown. If you have the wrong sort a hi-fi shop should be able to provide you with an adaptor.)

Assuming the recorder is properly connected, programs can be stored on a cassette by pressing the record and play buttons on the tape recorder and then typing a command on the computer to send the program. The recorder will then record the computer output as a series of bleeps. Some computers contain a 'motor control' which will switch the tape recorder's motor on when the program is about to be recorded and off when it has finished. A motor control is almost essential if, later on, you want to use the cassette recorder to store data as well as programs.

Every program you record on tape will need to have a name so that it can be identified and distinguished from other programs when you come to play it back. You need to give a name to the program at the time the command is given to the computer to send the program to the recorder. So if your program were the one to test a child's multiplication tables (from Chapter 4) you might want to call the program TABLES. The command typed in could be SAVE ''TABLES'' (followed by pressing of the RETURN button). The computer then sends the program to the recorder, preceded by a 'label' which in effect says 'this program is called TABLES'. It will take a short while for the program to be recorded on tape and the recorder should not be touched until everything has been sent. Some machines make a noise through the loudspeaker while the program is being recorded and the end of the program will correspond to the end of the noise. In most systems a visual prompt on the screen will tell you when the recording is finished.

In order to play back a program, run the tape back and type in the appropriate command – which might be LOAD ''TABLES'' and press return. The computer will tell you to play the tape and it then 'listens' to the tape until it finds a program labelled TABLES and then takes the program into its memory. If the program is not the first one on the tape the machine may well display on the screen the names of all the other programs it passes while looking for the one labelled TABLES. Once it has found and loaded the program the 'prompt' will appear and all you need to do is to type RUN and the program should work.

At this point it is worth pointing out that though the cassette recorder is a cheap and cheerful way of storing programs it is also a source of considerable frustration to many microcomputer owners. Sometimes tapes fail to play properly. The volume control on the recorder may need to be set at a very precise level before programs will load, crinkles in the tape may cause imperfect recording or playback, dirt on the playheads may cause trouble and it only needs one 'bit' of information to be incorrect for the program to fail to work. With practice, though, tapes can be made to work reasonably well and they are undoubtedly a cheap way of storing programs.

One major irritation caused by tapes is their slow speed. If you have a number of programs recorded on one tape it's impossible to find the right one by listening to the tape yourself.

To the human ear all tape recorded computer programs will sound alike – just a screeching noise – so the computer will have to look at each one on the tape until it finds the right one unless you have an idea of how far into the tape the program is, in which case you could run the tape to a position just before the program starts and run it from there. However, it is better to use short C12 cassettes for your programs – do not be tempted to use cheap C90 or C60 cassettes. If you do, two things happen. First, record or playback errors become common and second you could spend a long time looking for a program.

Sound, colour, graphics and movement

High resolution graphics on the screen (from a music applications program).

In Chapter 4 we looked at the simplest commands and instructions in BASIC which most dialects will understand. In the case of the more recent machines coming on the market, some of the exciting things which you can do involve the use of sound, colour and graphics, three areas where individual machines almost certainly differ from one another. Instructions like PLOT, COLOUR, DRAW and BEEP enable you to draw lines on the screen, produce different colours and make sounds of different pitch (if the computer has a loudspeaker).

Two examples of the kinds of program made possible by the use of these keywords are games involving collisons between moving objects on the screen and music programs, where it is possible to use the computer keyboard to compose music which appears as notes drawn on a musical stave created with graphics on the screen and which can then be played back as music through the computer's loudspeaker.

Other people's programs

One way of looking at the present microcomputer scene is to compare it with piano playing in the early days of the gramophone at the turn of the century. In those days, as now, a family might own a piano on which individual members of the household could learn to play and get pleasure from playing, however badly they did it. The same family could also buy the newly invented gramophone records (or cylinder recordings) of professional pianists and enjoy those as well. The present microcomputer scene is similar; individuals can get enjoyment and a feeling for computing by doing a little programming themselves – however badly. In the same way that some people become very proficient at playing the piano so some will become reasonably

good programmers. At the same time it is now easy to buy programs (applications programs) written by other people to run on your microcomputer. At present, rather like the early gramophone records, the programs are not very numerous and not always particularly good. However, just as the sophistication of the gramophone industry has grown over the years both in quantity and in the quality of what it offers, so the market for commercial microcomputer programs is likely to grow and their quality is likely to improve in the next few years.

Continuing our analogy, commercial gramophone recordings were supplemented in the late 1920s by the advent of broadcasting which provided a new and 'free' source of music. In the computer world similar developments may also not be far off. It is quite possible now to broadcast 'telesoftware' using the teletext services offered by the BBC and IBA and in a similar way to obtain computer programs down the telephone line using the Post Office's Prestel system. The truth is that these are early days.

The simplest commercial software which can be bought on audio cassette is loaded into the computer in the same way as programs you might write yourself. Problems arise if the software is written in a dialect of BASIC not recognised by your machine and this will continue to be a problem until there is some agreement over standardising BASIC itself. Other problems arise if the program is too long for the computer to handle because it fills up all its random-access memory. This brings us to the question of expanding the microcomputer system. Most microcomputers, other than the very cheapest, are capable of a good deal of expansion and of being able to link to a number of different 'peripherals'. Most of the examples of applications mentioned later in this chapter involve expanded systems, expanded in different ways depending on the application.

Memory expansion

Computer programs involving a lot of text use a good deal of memory and the first thing you may want in the way of expansion is to increase the memory of the machine from its initial 1K, 4K or 16K of random-access memory to a higher value. (K stands for kilo or thousand – well, nearly. 1K of memory is actually 1,024 bytes in the computer world, and 4K is 4,096 bytes [1024 is 2^{10} and 4096 is 2^{12} . . . and so on].) Some computers can have their memory expanded by simply having extra memory chips plugged in by a dealer: others may need an expansion box to be connected to the machine. To give you some idea of how much memory a program occupies, the route finding program in Chapter 4 occupies about 1.5K of random access memory.

Besides RAM expansion some computers also have the capacity to expand the amount of read-only memory (ROM). Remember that the ability of the computer to understand BASIC instructions depends on a BASIC interpreter chip held in ROM. Other languages can also be plugged in so that there is a choice for the user. Alternatively, applications programs which are going to be used often can be frozen onto ROM chips and these can be bought and plugged in. Word processing programs are a good example.

Peripheral devices

All kinds of devices can be connected to the computer to make it do different things if it has been designed to link up with them. Some are quite expensive compared with the computer itself and are only likely to be used in, say, a small business or professional application. The diagram overleaf shows some of the more important ones.

Disc drives

The disadvantages of the cassette recorder can be overcome by use of 'floppy disc' units (see page 88) which enable a much larger amount of information to be stored and found very quickly indeed. These discs are magnetically-coated discs of thin plastic which are held in protective envelopes. When they are inserted into the disc-drive housings they are able to rotate and can be read by a recording/replay 'head' which can move over the radius of the disc and either 'write' or 'read' information at any part of the disc.

Almost any serious application will require a disc drive unit or a pair of units and the cost of these and the electronics needed to link them with the computer will probably be more than the machine itself, though prices are expected to fall as more of them are sold. A good deal of business software is available on disc but it is very important to find out from a reliable, independent source what precisely is possible, what it is likely to cost and how well it works, before launching out into disc storage.

Using a 5" disc drive unit.
The removable panels beside the drive itself hide sockets for plugging in circuit cards which provide extra memory and other facilities.

143

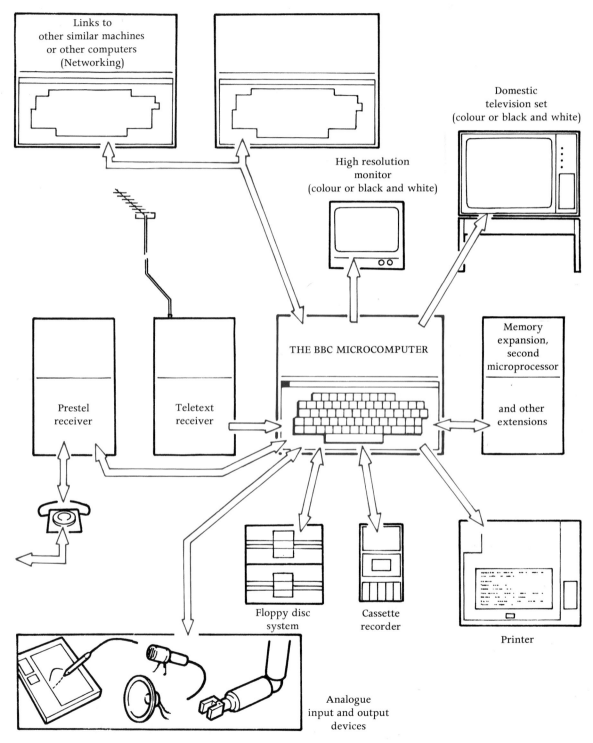

Links to
other similar machines
or other computers
(Networking)

Domestic
television set
(colour or black and white)

High resolution
monitor
(colour or black and white)

THE BBC MICROCOMPUTER

Memory
expansion,
second
microprocessor

and other
extensions

Prestel
receiver

Teletext
receiver

Floppy disc
system

Cassette
recorder

Printer

Analogue
input and output
devices

Printers

Printers can be quite cheap or very expensive, depending on the quality of the print you want to produce. If all you want to do is to keep a written copy of your computer programs (by asking the computer to send the listings to the printer) a 'thermal' printer would do. This uses a special heat sensitive paper which changes colour where a heated spot on a moving print head touches it.

An inexpensive thermal printer, right, which uses a special heat-sensitive paper.

Expanding the system.
Provided that the microcomputer has been designed to be expanded, a range of 'peripheral' devices can be linked to it. The most important of these are shown left.

Next in quality – and price – is a dot matrix printer (see page 93). This kind of printer can provide print of quite an acceptable quality for printing invoices and sheets of sales data. It uses ordinary paper.

The best quality printers are the 'daisy wheel' or 'thimble' printers used for word processing systems – in 1981, prices range from £1,200 upwards – produce impeccable quality print and can usually have interchangeable typefaces. Many of the printers on the market will run when connected to the microcomputer through a standard 'interface'. However, getting them to work properly and at the right speed initially may require the help of a technician – so, again, take advice.

Games paddles

Games paddles are 'joystick' devices which can be plugged in to some computers to enable you to play 'bat and ball' games on the screen. Many games can be played on the computer using the keyboard alone, so these games paddles are not essential if you want to use the computer for games.

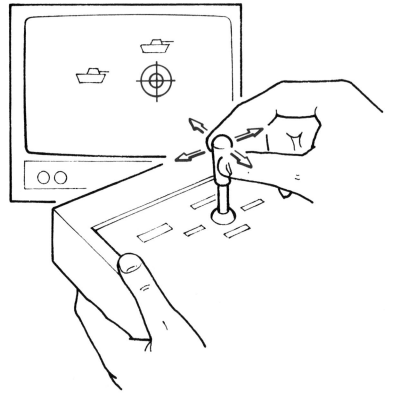

The 'joystick' control. Moving the top of the stick causes the symbols to move around the screen in a similar path.

Teletext and Prestel

Both broadcast teletext and the GPO's Prestel services are sources of a great variety of information which can be received and displayed on the television screen. Collectively they are referred to as 'viewdata'.

Teletext uses a hitherto unused part of the television signal to send digitally-coded information through the air; Prestel sends similar information down the telephone line and then through a special adaptor into a television receiver. Teletext is free but is only able to transmit information in one direction; Prestel costs the user the price of a telephone call with additional charges for some of the pages of information supplied but it is possible to send information in both directions along the telephone line, which means that Prestel is capable of two-way communication.

The digital data supplied by these services can be read by attaching decoding devices to the computer and can then be

Teletext.

Top – The digital information which makes up the BBC's Ceefax service is seen here as a row of dots which seem to 'run along' the top two lines of the television picture. A suitable decoder converts this into pages of text on the screen.

Middle – Ceefax editorial staff compiling pages – in this case an index and a financial page.

Below – A Ceefax page of 'Telesoftware' designed not to be read but to be loaded automatically into a suitably connected microcomputer, which can then run the program. This makes teletext capable of being a vehicle for 'interactive' material.

stored in the memory. The data could be straightforward information – like news, weather or stock market figures, or it could be an interactive computer program, in which case it is called *telesoftware*. Viewdata represents a way in which computer software will be distributed in the near future. Teletext will provide a free service; Prestel software could be commercial, paid for through the telephone bill.

Both Prestel and teletext are systems pioneered in Britain. The two systems have been developing independently but do use a common way of presenting information on the screen; the microcomputer with add-on teletext and Prestel decoders may be the means of bringing the systems together in a powerful new way.

Analogue input/output devices

How do you go about using your microcomputer to run your greenhouse, for example, or control a model train set or weigh a beehive (see page 75)? If you plan to try this sort of thing, then you will need a machine with at least one input/output 'port' – a connection point for adding input or output devices to the machine. This allows information to be sent to and from the computer in the binary form used by the processor, and thus lets you connect or 'interface' all sorts of things to the computer.

Simple devices like switches need little interfacing as they are essentially binary devices. Thus burglar alarm systems lend themselves easily to computer control. In the other direction, equipment can be switched on and off fairly simply by signals – suitably amplified – coming from the computer. Computer systems with internal timers or clocks obviously help here.

If other signals need to be handled, special interfaces like analogue-digital converters are needed. Sometimes these are built into the microcomputer – we saw in Chapter 3 (page 93) how these convert varying voltages into equivalent digital signals, as required by the computer. This makes it possible for it, for example, both to simulate sound and to manipulate and process it.

Computers with the right analogue input/output devices can be used to control, and get information to and from various instruments like temperature sensors or weighing devices. Thus they can become intelligent controllers in, say, a laboratory.

There is a great deal of emphasis (particularly in education) on making use of the computer to control things, so it is very likely that the next few years will see a variety of control sensors and activators coming on to the market.

Chickens weighing in.
A microcomputer application in farming. As each bird hops on to the perch its weight is recorded by the computer. In this way the computer builds up a complete picture of the spread of their weights. This can help the farmer (or the computer) to judge how much food to give and when the birds are ready for market.

What can microcomputers be used for?

One very common area of application for microcomputers is playing games. We have become familiar with computer-based games in the amusement arcade – 'space invaders' is a good example – though more conventional games like noughts and crosses, chess, draughts, bridge and backgammon have also been adapted for the microcomputer. Games will become more popular, since many of the newer microcomputers – especially those aimed at home use – have good graphics, usually in colour. Most games involve the use of graphics, probably using a colour or black and white television screen.

Many of the games involving objects moving fast across the screen or involving a great deal of calculation on the part of the computer (like chess) have programs written in low-level machine language, but many of the others are written in BASIC. Books of BASIC games programs are on the market and some of them even help you write your own.

Stretching the mind. Computers at a chess tournament.

Games are not only for amusement. It is quite fashionable among so-called computer experts to run down the playing of games on a computer. Most microcomputer users will tell you that one of the easiest and most pleasant ways of learning how to program is to get hooked on a game, want to learn how it works and then try to write your own. Among the reasons given by many computer professionals for joining computer clubs is that it is not possible to play games on the computer at work! If your prospective computer is to be used in the home it most certainly must have a games capability. This could mean an ability to have games 'joysticks' attached, and possibly sound output. The joystick allows the operator to move graphic symbols on the screen and some form of sound output adds that extra 'something'.

Computer games can also be 'mind stretching'. Most desktop systems can now play a passable game of chess, backgammon or bridge, or other games of strategy. Many of the computer magazines devote a large proportion of their editorial space to games programs, and this is a cheap and easy way to keep your library up to date with the latest developments.

The great thing about the microcomputer is its interactive nature. The computer will usually prove a worthy opponent, at whatever level of difficulty you agree on!

Educating yourself

Computer-aided learning programs are available that can help with maths, physics, French, English and even computer programming. Now that equipment is becoming cheaper, schools and colleges are able to buy a computer for a modest amount of money. Even where budgets are being slashed, the computer seems high on the list of most schools' equipment requirements. Unfortunately the use of machines in schools is still limited by the lack of good software and the lack of teachers trained in their use. Cheap computers, though, can be bought by students and used in the home, and this is where a lot of parents will meet them for the first time.

English primary school children with a low-cost commercial spelling tester.

Those people who have been in the microcomputer business since it began – about five years – like to compare the impact and projected numbers of microcomputers to those of the pocket calculator. The availability of cheap pocket calculators has had a profound effect on the teaching of mathematics and science. Similar things are happening with computers and the impact on all areas of teaching could be enormous.

There are several types of program used in education:

1 drill and practice
2 tutorials
3 simulation or modelling
4 a combination of these four.

Drill and practice programs are used to help the student master a skill he has already been taught but which needs practice. We

151

saw a simple example earlier with the child's 'times table' test in Chapters 2 and 4. On a much larger scale, in many of the schools in Dallas, Texas, for example, microcomputers are used regularly in the classroom to reinforce the teaching of a whole range of primary maths skills. Students get tired or frustrated with this kind of program if they have to sit at the computer too long but they can be very useful, particularly if they free the teacher to do other things. In Dallas, each child gets about 15 minutes of concentrated activity each day on the computer. The programs, written by the teachers themselves, make use of a wide variety of techniques on the screen. The computers address each child by name and can be programmed to test speed as well as accuracy, keeping a record of the child's performance which the teachers can refer to later.

Tutorial programs are designed to teach subjects to students by providing them with pages of information and diagrams and then checking if they have understood by asking questions. If the answers are right the student gets directed one way; if they are wrong he gets directed another, possibly having the information presented a different way. These program-learning techniques have some limited value for particular groups of students needing to learn quite specific bodies of knowledge, computer programming itself being a good example.

An eight-year-old Dallas schoolboy working on one of the many maths programs written by the teachers of the city.

A Student at London's Royal College of Art working on a graphics tutorial program.

Simulation or modelling programs deal with real-world events which can be mimicked on the television screen. It is not necessary for the user physically to encounter the actual problem because data collected from the real world is often entered into the programs; the main aim is to develop decision-making skills as well as understanding.

Good examples are found in science where, for example, students can perform experiments in chemistry and make predictions about the results of certain actions without the need to touch any apparatus. In physics, a circuit diagram can be presented on the screen together with questions asking what would happen if particular switches were closed or certain components introduced. In another example, a simple simulation shows how gas molecules move around inside a box. By using the keyboard the student can see what happens to the molecules if the box is heated or compressed or a hole appears in its side.

A 'ballistics' simulation game. Enemies on each side of the hill fire missiles at each other, into or against the 'wind'. Those playing the game have to estimate the angle of fire and the fire power needed to land on and thus blow up the opponent.

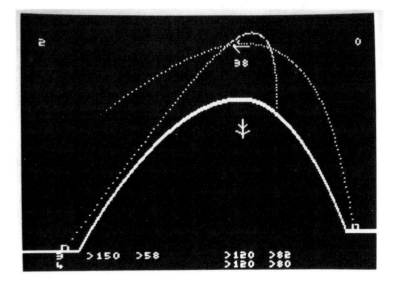

One popular program starts with the words, 'If you stand on a tall enough mountain and if you throw an object fast enough, it will go into orbit.' Then the program asks you for your values of elevation and velocity, and calculates what happens. Another program shows planetary motion and the size and relative positions of the planets in the solar system. The program can be made to simulate planetary motion between any two dates in history.

Language teaching has not been forgotten, and most common languages are catered for. In Russian, for example, a program introduces you to the Cyrillic alphabet, and then takes you through simple grammar and vocabulary problems. Most language programs are designed to teach vocabulary and grammar, but pronunciation will have to wait until good speech synthesis and recognition are implemented.

To help teachers, special 'authoring' languages are being designed. These allow pages of information, containing both graphics and text, to be constructed far more easily than BASIC allows. Decision points may be programmed so that correct and wrong answers lead to different 'frames'. Whole programs may be written using these languages and then recorded, like BASIC programs, for later use. Author languages may be considered as the next stage in the hierarchy of high-level languages.

Games programs are fun, as we have said, and educational games that are well designed help students to develop their thinking. Although there are thousands of these programs around, software development has not kept up with advances in hardware and the software that is available is fairly poor at the moment, although there are some good programs available in maths and science. This is to be expected, of course, but it is only a matter of time before programs get better, as more and more teachers gain experience in the use of computers.

Business games are quite popular in management studies. The student is given all the information to allow him to make decisions about how to run a business. 'Chance' events like a fire, or sudden changes in commodity prices or interest rates, can be built in.

For younger children, probably the most popular teaching 'game' is a computerised version of Hangman. You can usually choose the level of difficulty, and how many wrong guesses are allowed before a gibbet and cartoon 'man' appear on the screen. Some of the better versions allow the teacher to change the word-list, so that groups of words relevant to the class can be used.

Hangman
Guess one of the remaining letters correctly and it will appear in the word. Fail, or spend too long thinking about it, and the gibbet man will be completed and your game will be lost.

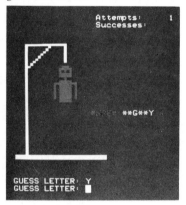

Business applications

When we come to consider the commercial use of microcomputers, the options are many and varied. Even at the domestic level, finance programs exist for keeping a check on your bank balance, calculating income tax returns, as an address and telephone file, diary-keeping and even cataloguing books and records.

In a commercial environment, the investment of a few thousand pounds will usually pay for itself in one year. American studies have shown that any company with a turnover greater than £100,000 p.a. is losing money by not having a computer.

This does not mean that even smaller companies would not benefit from computerisation. Book-keeping is an obvious job for a computer. Large and medium-sized companies already make extensive use of computer technology, but microcomputers now make it possible for even small companies (including one-man businesses) to rationalise their book-keeping, order processing, current-account ledgers, invoicing, salaries, stock accounting, budget and so on. People who have invested in microcomputers include doctors, consultants, shopkeepers, stockbrokers, garage proprietors and people running restaurants and hotels. However, relatively simple microcomputer systems will not achieve much. With business applications, the main factor governing the choice of a system is not what the company is doing now, but what it is going to be doing in three or five years time. Thus 'expandability' has to be considered in a major purchase.

Inside 'The Chocolate Box'
Phyllis Arrandale was introduced to computing only two years ago. She taught herself to write her own programs and now finds the equipment invaluable in running her small business because, as she points out, it enables her to know her exact financial position at any time.

Word processing

For the system to work in a rational and convenient manner, it needs a lot of storage and this is the limiting factor in many microcomputer systems. Above all, well written – and easily modifiable – software is needed.

After business accounting, word processing and information handling are the two most common uses of computers in the office, and both are being revolutionised by the microcomputer.

It may be simple enough to write a letter, but typing an attractive and faultless text is difficult for most of us, unless we are trained

155

The word processor.
This microcomputer doubles as an accounting system and a word processor. Foreground – a high quality printer prints out a letter.

typists. A word processing system can be built around a cheap microcomputer to make the whole procedure much simpler and reduce frustration. Word processing essentially means that you type the text in the normal way on a keyboard connected to the computer, the text appearing on a screen and not on paper. With the assistance of the computer, you then correct and edit the text until it is exactly as you want it. After this, the computer linked to a printer supplies a perfect printout, with as many copies as needed, and the text can even be stored for later use usually on a disc – though cassettes can be used. Specially-written word processing software enables you to produce the text on the screen on command, to correct spelling errors, erase, add, exchange sentences or paragraphs and get a printed output.

Typical word processors automatically break the text up into lines as you type. There is no need to hit RETURN at the end of a line. The preceding line is re-displayed 'justified' to the left and right margins. Lines can be centred with one keystroke, and set in bold typeface or underlined in mid-paragraph. The text can even be re-justified to new margins when necessary. Page headings and page numbers can easily be entered and pauses between pages and headings can be inserted during printing.

As an example of how you can use your own word processing system, let us look at letters. For each letter, you have to type in your rough copy, edit it on the screen until you are satisfied, and then get a copy printed. If you have a large number of letters that are basically the same, you can also input an address list of the people who are to be sent the letters. In this way each letter will appear to be a personal one, despite the fact that the printout has been done with the aid of the computer. You can even store a number of standard phrases which can be called up when needed and put together, for example in a contract.

Many letters we receive today have been addressed by a computer. The microcomputer can be used in the same way as large commercial computers to produce letters like these, and for storing, updating and printing names and addresses. It may be a list of members or customers – or perhaps even a list of Christmas cards to be sent.

A word processing system can also be used for keeping mailing lists. A good mailing list program should contain search routines, to make it possible to find a certain person in the register, or to print out all those who live in a particular geographical area, or to sort in alphabetical order and so on.

Professional word processing systems can cost anything up to £10,000 or even more. Using a microcomputer with a word processing program allows you to get a long way for considerably less, although the range of facilities is limited. The peripherals must include a good quality keyboard for inputting the text, and a good quality output device such as a daisy-wheel, or similar quality of printer (see page 45). The printer is the part that costs money, especially if you want attractively laid-out copy with a good quality typescript.

Stock control

Many small companies keep track of their stock with a microcomputer. A computerised stock control system is usually combined with order entry and order invoicing. One aim is to minimise the errors in copying the invoice to the stock record. Stock balances tend to be more accurate if invoices are produced immediately after goods are issued. Information about orders can be made available quickly and, when required, the system should be able to produce predictions about the chances of running out of stock based on its past experience.

Stock control is one of the most important functions of a computer in small, and large, businesses. The information base built up allows not only the prediction of feasible future events, but also 'modelling' of the business for forecasting and future planning. When linked in with payroll accounting, sales and purchase ledger, a powerful system can be developed for the efficient and profitable running of the business.

Distribution

A number of companies are now using microcomputers to organise the most efficient methods for distributing products around the country. The programs include road network analysis to calculate the quickest route around the distribution network, as well as warehouse and depot locations. Coupled with account 'clustering', these programs can be integrated into a total planning system.

Computers in the warehouse of a small company.
They provide for the easy processing of orders and invoices and an accurate record of all the stock in hand at any one time.

Groups of independent lorry drivers have come together to organise one computer-based information system. A central office connects with computers at various points around the country and customers with loads to be carried can telephone in locally with their requirements. The local computers display the information relevant to that area and plan the drivers' routes accordingly. Information on the cheapest fuel distributors on the chosen route is also available. Wherever the driver is, he can find out what work is available locally and, together with the other information, he can make the most efficient use of his vehicle.

Controlling things

The application of computers to control things is one of the most interesting and developing areas for using the microcomputer. A modest system *could* be used as an aid to piano tuning, to monitor and control an experiment in a laboratory or to control the sluices, water levels and gates in a canal lock. Model railway buffs are beginning to use microcomputers to control trains and track layouts. One simple circuit will control 16 trains and 128 sets of points, for example. The potential list is endless. The main challenges, though, are not usually with the computer itself or even with the programs needed to get it to do the job – they are the problems associated with getting meaningful information into and out of the computer from the real world.

Opening up a new possibility. The automatic operation of canal locks is technically perfectly feasible. Whether or not the capital investment would make it worthwhile and whether as a result most of the fun would be taken out of a canal holiday remains to be seen.

Take an imaginary (but perfectly possible) canal lock control program, for example. This could contain some fairly simple reflection in BASIC of obvious instructions such as 'if the lock is full, open the upstream gates and close the upper sluices'. If you have understood the basic principles of problem solving and programming you should now see how this kind of program could be tackled.

The challenge comes when we try to *measure* whether the lock is full or not and to *get* a lock gate to open. This involves sensing devices and activators which need to trigger or be triggered by the computer. In fact the lock gates problem is not too difficult: a float could operate a switch when the lock is full and a motor could open the gates. A switch is either open or closed and a motor is either switched on or off, so here it is relatively easy to get the computer, which deals in 1s and 0s (on and off) to communicate with either of them through some simple circuitry. This would, for example, use the low voltage signals of the computer to control the more powerful supply needed for the motor for the lock gates and sluices. These, in their turn, would need other sensors to tell the computer when they were fully open so that it could switch the motors off.

The electronic
piano tuner

On page 70 we described the simple way in which an electronic piano tuner could do the job. In terms of the basic ideas it's easy enough to understand but it's not so easy in practice. Again, the problems arise when we get the sound from the piano and convert it into a form the computer can cope with. A microphone could pick up the sound, producing electrical signals which would need converting from their analogue (continuously varying) form into a digital representation. An 'analogue to digital converter' would be needed between the microphone and the computer. The computer could 'sample' the waveform of the incoming sound and compare the frequency with a figure held in its memory. The results – too high, too low or the same – would determine how an output device behaved. This could be a screen which says whether the frequency is right or not and would be the simplest kind of output. The human piano tuner could then tighten or loosen the string accordingly until the frequency was exact. More ambitious ideas for an output device which involves a special kind of motor turning the tuning pegs are easy to describe but are more difficult to realise. An enormous 'twist' would be needed to overcome the friction holding the peg in its hole. However, it is a possibility.

Future years will see more and more ingenious control applications as the microcomputer becomes surrounded by a variety of reliable peripherals suitable for linking it with the real world.

Computers for the disabled

Small computer systems are changing not only the way disabled people look at the world, but also how the world looks at the disabled. Advances in speech recognition are beginning to do away with the need for a keyboard. The ability to use highly complicated equipment with little movement by the operator has opened up completely new areas of work.

For example, it is possible for a severely disabled and dumb person to control a machine, which makes audible sounds, with just a toe. The control mechanism – which looks like a stick – has 80 different positions. Some represent words and numbers. Most are sounds and parts of words, and by moving the stick to different positions, the user can construct sentences which the computer then 'speaks'.

Computers for the disabled
'Mavis'. Using a foot operated joystick-type of control, this severely disabled boy can move the cursor along the alphabet displayed at the bottom of the screen and choose his letter for a hangman game.

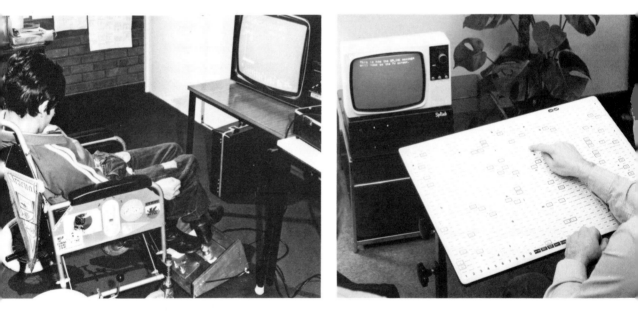

Right:
'Splink' which enables a person with a speech disability to create words and sentences on the screen using a touch-sensitive keyboard. The keyboard contains some common complete words (with black borders) but mainly separate syllables, used as building blocks.

If more movement of the body is possible, there is another computer-related development. This system consists of a small wordboard with around 950 commonly used words in alphabetical order. The user depresses the appropriate words on the keyboard, which is usually on the lap, and builds them into sentences which appear on an associated screen. An infra-red link between the wordboard and the processor gets rid of loose, trailing wires. There are individual letters on the wordboard which allow individual words to be constructed, as well as the key-codes which allow whole phrases to be used by only touching one key.

Finally, a couple of unusual examples.

Bee keeping

In the West of Ireland a commercial apiary uses a small computer system to keep track of its bees. The program ensures that a master record is kept on each hive and its environment. This includes information such as the height of the hive above ground, the make of hive, the material from which it's constructed, the nature of the surrounding countryside and so on. As all these factors affect the welfare of the bees and consequently their honey, a careful record is required. Up to 100 variables can be fed into the system. The input can be amended to account for such major changes as change of Queen, diet or location and the records can be updated for production changes and other brood data. A print-out from the computer provides a daily work schedule showing which hives are to be inspected, their diet, and other points to be checked. Incidentally, all input and output is in Gaelic!

Still on the subject of bees, a school science laboratory in the Midlands is aiming to use a microcomputer linked to an electronic weighing device to weigh a hive every few seconds and keep track of the results. In this way the pupils will be able to study the comings and goings of the bees to see if there is any pattern to their activity.

Newsagents

A number of newsagents are now using computers to schedule the delivery boys' rounds. One company in the West country has 3,500 customers, and each morning and evening the paperboys receive printed delivery lists. Each list is personalised and takes account of the day of the week and the papers ordered. The main benefits of the system include increased accuracy, reduced clerical work and wastage of papers and a reduction in the number of outstanding paper bills. The customers get their papers earlier and the newsagent has a little longer in bed each morning!

Choosing a system

It is very difficult to give advice which will satisfy every prospective buyer of a microcomputer system. All the examples above use different systems with different peripherals and different software programs.

The very cheapest microcomputers on the market are ideal if you simply want to find out a little about computing – but they have their limitations. If you have a serious application in mind or you feel that you might develop a long term interest, it's probably best to buy a system which is capable of expansion and which has a good, robust keyboard. However, to make a sensible choice the best thing to do is to take advice.

Advice Reading the computer press is a good idea. There are now a number of magazines on the market catering for the personal computer owner which will give some idea of the range of equipment available. However, the first time buyer may well be baffled by the hyperbole of the advertisements and the technical language used in the articles reviewing equipment.

High-street computer shops exist, though many of them are agents for particular makes of computer and therefore may not be impartial in their advice. Nonetheless, they should be able to demonstrate equipment and be able to discuss the availability of software with you. The problem for many first time buyers is that it is not easy to know what questions to ask and it is easy to be impressed by demonstrations. But don't be afraid to say if you don't understand the technical sales talk. A well established local shop with a good reputation and knowledgeable staff may be a very good place to 'get your eye in'. Micro systems centres and other small advice centres – some run by public bodies like the National Computer Centre – are springing up, able to give impartial professional advice to, for example, the small business man. Computer clubs exist and again, although individuals in them are usually enthusiasts and very evangelical about computing and about the equipment they themselves have bought, they can be helpful sources of advice. Ideally, advice can best

The Birmingham Micro Centre – one of an increasing number of places where prospective buyers can try out standard business and educational packages.

come from people who have bought equipment for a particular purpose similar to the one you may have in mind. One final source of advice could be a local school or college which has a computer studies department.

Some questions to ask:

1   Is the system easy to use – as far as you can see? Does the manufacturer have a good reputation?
2   Is the manual comprehensible, with a good index?
3   Can it be used at home on trial, without obligation to buy?
4   Is there a local source of advice about how to use the system if you get into difficulty? What about servicing arrangements?
5   Is the system well supported with applications programs?
6   Does it have a reasonable amount of random-access memory? Up to 4K will not support a long program; 16K will support a substantial applications program, but more will be needed if a lot of text data is to be stored. Can additional memory be plugged neatly in to the machine or does it require an expansion box?
7   Does the machine support low, medium and/or high resolution graphics, sound, colour?

b 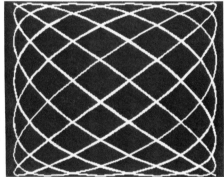   c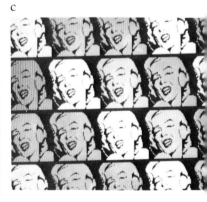

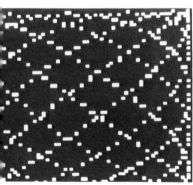

Low, medium and high resolution graphics.
a) 'Chunky' graphics, made up of fairly large square 'picture cells'. For the computer's memory to 'map' all the pattern on the screen it needs '1K' of space.
b) The same pattern in a higher resolution, this time needing '10K' of space. The picture cells are much smaller.
c) High resolution, using '20K' of memory space.

8   Will the machine link easily to a range of peripherals like printers, a disc system or viewdata?
9   Will the machine accept plug-in ROM chips for specific applications programs or extra languages?
10 Is the system capable of linking with other computers or with a second microprocessor for future expansion?

Above all, the question to ask yourself is – what do you want to do with the computer?

One way of beginning might be to buy a cheap system and then, having exhausted its possibilities, sell it and buy something better. Alternatively you may find you have exhausted your own interest, in which case you won't have wasted much money.

Another aspect to consider is that computing can become addictive, as many a spouse has discovered as his or her partner clacks away on the keyboard, deep into the night.

Earning money

Some computer users consider the possibility of earning some money the most important reason for buying a system. There is a lack of really good software at the moment, and this is the first area to consider if you have a 'forte' for programming. If you're good at it then the purchase of a well known and popular system could be the key to a prosperous future! Some people are now making a living writing software for the major software distributors. As these companies usually work on a straight royalty basis, 10% on a £10 program works out at a reasonable amount even if only 10 a week are sold!

Many local retailers, unfortunately, do not have the software expertise they need. Tailoring, or altering existing programs so that they meet a specific, slightly different need, is a starting point. If you are an accountant, for example, with programming ability then your local retailer will probably welcome you with open arms.

You could advertise. The computer magazines usually have cheap advertising space for the one man band. You could even contact your local computer clubs, since people with software problems will contact them for help.

As more and more educational institutions now have computers, it is becoming easier to get a background in computer programming. Similarly, the engineering industry is becoming more and more computer orientated, and anybody with a talent for electronics or programming (not necessarily mathematicians, either) should consider a career in one or more areas of computing – as a country we only produce about half the graduates industry needs in digital electronics.

6 The limits to growth

What the computer can't (yet) do

By now we should be far enough up the hillside of knowledge to be able to turn round and take a broad view over the landscape, in order to see what computers can, and what they can't do. What do we want them to do? Well, the human race being the lazy object it is perhaps would like computers to do all the tiring and monotonous things of life, while we do the amusing, interesting and creative ones!

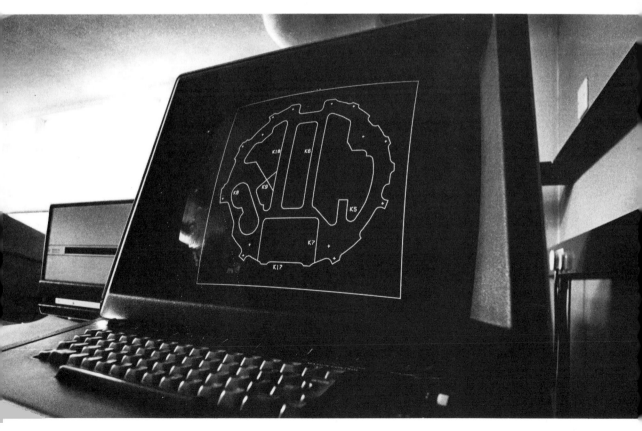

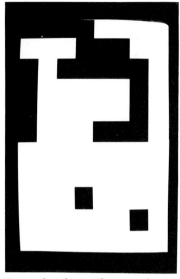

Guess what this is. There are about 100 'bits' of information in the picture.

Making a living in the modern industrialised state tends to mean that you sit at a desk or a cash register, stand at a lathe, sit in the cockpit of an aircraft or at the wheel of a car. You are asked, first of all, to understand what is put before you. That involves, firstly, either seeing or hearing. This bit of paper is an invoice for £342.96. Over there is a road sign saying 'M1 and the North'. The altimeter reads 15,000 feet and air traffic control is telling me to climb to level 27. The phone rings and a voice says, 'Please bring the Mutronics file to the Boardroom'. A trolley is wheeled up, full of engineering parts – you have to drill 43 rivet holes, one-eighth of an inch diameter, in specified positions. And so on.

It is just at this basic stage that at present the computer fails us. We can't yet make it see as we see, or hear as we hear. The computer may be stupid, but it is not lazy. We can tell it to reconcile all our accounts, in one snap of the central processor. But we are not doing nearly so well in teaching it to see, to hear, or even to speak. To understand why, we have to take a look at the information *we* process when we carry out what to us are these simple activities.

Teaching the computer English

The same 'picture' but with 400 'bits'.

The 26 letters of the alphabet combine to make some 15 million permissible English words, let alone those in French, Spanish, German and Yashmak. Simply to test a word to see if it is a proper English word means looking for it in this 15 million word dictionary.

The computer can do this, but so far we have concentrated on teaching it to do it the logical way – the sort of way we used to find Mr Brznski in the telephone book on page 32. In other words, we tell it to test the first letter of the suspect word against the first letter of the first word in the dictionary. If it matches, to test the second, if it fails, to test the first letter against the first letter of the second word. And so on, and so on. The amount of computing goes up in proportion to the number of possible words in the language.

Even at the speeds at which the central processor works, that means it is an incredible task even to check one single word. (In practice, programs that check spellings use a much more restricted dictionary.) However, this is only the first part of the problem for as soon as we combine these words into sentences we create a vast new family of symbols – that is, complete sentences. For instance: 'I'll meet you in the other place' and 'I'll meet you in the other plaice' are two different sentences. Only one letter has

With 1,600 'bits' – the picture is now recognisably a face. But whose?

been altered from the first to the second, but that single letter completely changes the meaning – or rather, reduces the sentence to gibberish. How do we explain to the computer why the second sentence is gibberish? 'Plaice' is a noun, after all, just like 'place'.

Of course, we could tell the computer to check sentences the logical way, too – by putting into its 'dictionary' every conceivable meaningful sentence, and telling it to check 'I'll meet you in the other plaice' to see if it is one of them. The volume of sentences we'd have to include is vast. For instance, if we reckon that the ordinary person uses about 10,000 words in sentences less than 30 words long, we would have to include some $10,000^{30}$ sentences (that's a 10 with 120 0s after it). Discs hold a lot of information, true, but that volume of text would fill 10^{115} (10 with 115 0s) discs!

Clearly, logical methods aren't going to get us far. We must take a lateral short cut and though computer people have some ideas in this direction, they haven't solved that problem yet.

. . . and to listen to us

With 6,400 'bits'.

The problem becomes even greater when we expect the computer not to read, but to listen to us. Before it can even start on this mammoth task of working out whether what we are saying makes sense (and we haven't even thought yet about how it might work out just what that sense means), it has to work out just what on earth it was we said.

We all tend to speak sloppily and our language, too, is easily misunderstood. There are plenty of words which sound the same, sometimes are even spelt the same, but have different meanings. We usually have no trouble ourselves in working out which word, or which meaning, is being used in a particular sentence. The construction and meaning of the sentence give us plenty of clues to go by. Indeed, we make so much use of the clues that if the person talking to us makes a verbal slip we often don't even notice – we 'hear' what we were expecting to hear. The computer doesn't have that advantage, though. It is not made that way.

Let's take another example. In order to conserve 'bandwidth', the telephone system cuts out the high frequencies – above 3,000 vibrations per second – in peoples' voices. As a result the sounds that come down the wire for, say, 'seven' and 'heaven' are actually identical. Yet we, listening at the other end, are very seldom confused. We have been cued beforehand that the speaker is going to refer to numbers or to theological concepts,

167

The 'paperless' electronic office may be just round the corner (this one uses a British computer system), but we are still a long way from the time when speech can be recognised reliably by the ordinary computer.

and our mental interpreter is ready and waiting at the appropriate spot in our vast mental store to compare what comes in with a range of appropriate possibilities.

Big mind – little computer

Lateral thinking aside, it is still true that our brains are a lot more powerful than a computer when it comes to finding and comparing information in this way. Inside our heads we have room for so many bits of information that, using the most advanced and compact technology available today, storing that volume of information would take a computer the size of the Albert Hall. Having stored it, what could the computer do with it? Certainly the human ability to jump around in this huge store of information, using very feeble clues, is something the computer can't yet begin to touch. When you see a face in the crowd and recognise a childhood friend of 30 years ago, and deduce from his appearance quite a lot about his life since you last saw him, that is something computers cannot start to imitate. Well, it's not so much that computers can't think of doing it – it's that we can't begin to think how to make them do it. As we said in Chapter 2, computers don't solve problems for us, they just carry out our solutions. And getting the computer to understand the language we write and speak is a problem we haven't yet solved.

168

Teaching the computer to see

Another problem we haven't yet solved is that of teaching the computer to understand what it sees, in the sort of way that we do. Getting the computer to see creates no problem – a video camera can simply be connected to one of its input ports. However getting it to make *sense* of what it sees is more difficult.

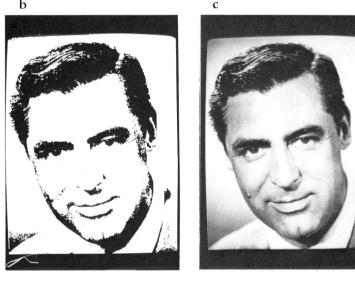

a

b

c

a
Left with 25,600 'bits'. Some people can recognise the face by now. Try it with your friends: would it help them to know that it was a film star?

b
With 102,400 'bits'.

c
With 409,600 'bits'. *It's Cary Grant* – but could the computer recognise him? How could we begin to explain to it how to recognise an individual?

Let us just consider the problem of recognising Cary Grant, let alone reproducing the way he walks and talks. Suppose that you can recognise him from, say, 10,000 other people you might see on your television screen, and that you can do this when his image occupies a quarter of the screen for five seconds. Now, a television picture consists of six hundred lines with about 600 coloured dots on each line – 360,000 dots altogether. Each dot can be one of three colours, and can have several different brightnesses. It turns out that it takes about six million bits, or nearly a million bytes, to hold the information contained in a complete television frame. Frames are repeated 25 times a second, so the information *we* need to identify Cary Grant is contained in $250,000 \times 5 \times 25 = 31$ million bytes and all this before we have worked out a way for the *computer* to begin to do the same thing.

It would still have to pick out Cary Grant from the other 9,999 people the picture might show. If we were to store the information needed to do this on hard disc, it would take an hour a heac just to read the data that defines our image of Cary Grant. And then, how would the computer know how the essence of Cary Grant is hidden in those 31 million bytes that identify him to us?

These figures are very rough, but they help to illustrate what cannot be done with today's hardware and software.

First steps

Daunting though the task is, the business of sound and vision input and output for computers is a major area for research in computer applications today. Let's take a brief look at some of the ways in which the research has met with success.

We have already seen how the computer can handle words, even if it does not understand what they mean. It can check their spelling, too, against a list of words it has been given. Though the number of words in the English language is so massive, most of us use only a small proportion of them. The computer can work with a 'dictionary' containing a few thousand words, including the sort of common words that appear in this chapter, and a special selection of technical words used in the area in which it is being applied, say, medical terms in a medical secretary's spelling program. It can also be fed a list of proper nouns that will frequently come up – the names of clients, towns in the area in which the firm using the program operates and so on. If a word in the text being checked does not appear in the dictionary, the program will alert the operator, and he or she will then need to check to see if it is a perfectly valid word that has not been included in the dictionary, or if it is actually a misspelling.

In the chapter on programming we saw how the computer uses certain words as commands; it understands these words and acts on what they tell it to do. The number of commands the computer will recognise is much smaller than the number of words in our dictionaries above, and this type of small selection of words has proved a good place to start teaching the computer to understand the spoken word.

Computers have begun to learn to 'hear' by repeatedly analysing the voice of one speaker, speaking a small selection of command words. The sound is first converted to electrical signals by a microphone. Then these analogue signals are converted into the binary pattern which the computer can recognise. After a number of repetitions they can distinguish the binary representation of, say, 'RUN', from the binary representation of 'LIST', or some other word in their vocabulary – and then act on the command in the same way as if it had been entered into the computer through a keyboard.

We saw earlier how this type of development is proving particularly useful for the handicapped. Steady improvements

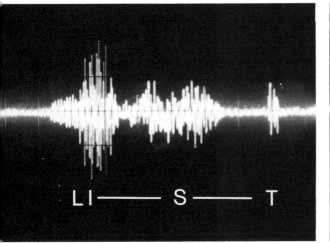
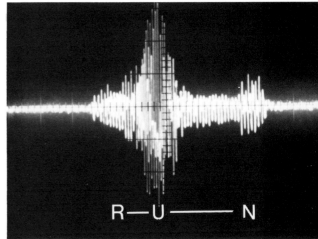

A visual representation of the soundwaves for the words 'LIST' (left above), and 'RUN' (right below), as seen on an oscilloscope screen. The patterns are clearly different and can easily be 'digitised'. If this kind of information is entered into the computer it will need to be able to match the received pattern with one of a number of patterns stored in its memory if it is to recognise a word.

have meant that the more advanced machines can now understand virtually any speaker and that their vocabularies are expanding slowly.

Teaching the computer to speak is not nearly so difficult. It can say virtually anything if its memory contains a suitable digital representation of what it is to say, and if it has a suitable output through which to say it. Some systems concentrate on teaching the computer the sounds of various syllables, which it then combines into words (sometimes rather odd Dalek-sounding words, admittedly); some teach it the entire word, or link it to a recording of a human being saying the word.

The first speaking word processors, which tell the typist what he or she has typed in (particularly useful for blind typists), and the first 'spelling test' machines, which say a word and then ask a child to enter its spelling, are already available.

Though the computer can't recognise Cary Grant yet, it is having a little success in recognising more simple patterns or objects. The first areas in which this type of vision recognition are being tried include the use of 'intelligent' machines, or robots, to sort simple parts. The computer has to learn to distinguish, say, a half inch rivet from a quarter inch bolt, whatever angle its input camera views them at. Even that is not easy, but it has taken some tentative steps in the right direction.

In yet other applications, we have found a more lateral way of thinking around the problem of the computer's limitations. Take that bar coding example we discussed in Chapter 1, for instance. The computer is doing much the same job as a shop assistant who picks up a tin of beans and thinks, 'Ah, yes, beans went up 1p this week'. Instead of recognising the picture of beans on the tin, though, the computer recognises the bar code, a convenient form of binary information which tells it that the tin contains beans, just as the picture on the tin tells the human assistant the same thing.

Practical problems

The computer is not quite as clever as all that! However, there are still plenty of jobs which don't demand these recognition skills, which we might think the computer would be extremely good at but for which it isn't yet being used.

Sometimes that's because we haven't yet got around to using the computer, but often it is because practical problems, quite unconnected with the business of getting the computer to process the information, step in to make using the computer impracticable. Let's look at some of these reasons why the microcomputer hasn't yet taken over from us.

Taking over drudgery – a termite in the works

We need to go back to when we first talked about what the microcomputer could do, in Chapter 1. We said that the computer's real forte was in taking over drudgery: doing boring, routine jobs that human beings don't enjoy and are not particularly good at. And that's true. But in fact, lots of jobs which we think of as routine are not really that straightforward after all.

For instance, a legal publishing firm got itself computerised. Part of its business was in sending heavy legal tomes to subscribing solicitors informing them of changes in the law. Part of the computer's job was to make up a delivery note for each lawyer, print an address label, and calculate the postage. All very fine and large, except for one particular subscriber who lived several hundred miles up the river Volta in central Africa. His books had to wait up to a fortnight in a riverside trading post for a boat going up-river. While they were there, they were subject to the attentions of some law-loving termites.

Dear old Winnie, or whoever had been in the Post Room before the computer, knew that this particular consignment had to be wrapped in lead foil if it were to arrive uneaten. The postage had to be increased by an appropriate amount. This had always been done – until the computer came, and the customer got several boxes of dust at £200 a time.

You might think that an office cleaner's job, say, was an example of pure drudgery. But, in fact, it requires very complex skills in recognising what is rubbish and what isn't. The human

Robots in Industry
Teaching a robot how to spray vitreous enamel on to cooker liners. Once the man has gone through the motions the robot can repeat them because it will have mapped the movements in its memory.

Robots in Industry

Top – Most robots are used for predictable, well-defined jobs in unpleasant conditions.

Below – Visual recognition robots are still at a relatively primitive stage of development. This is a laboratory scale machine designed to recognise the shape of a particular metal part and pick it up, no matter what position it is in. Parts are fed down the chute (left), on to an illuminated table. A camera, (top), looks at the part and feeds information into the computer, which recognises its shape and position and turns the table round so that an arm can come down and pick the piece up.

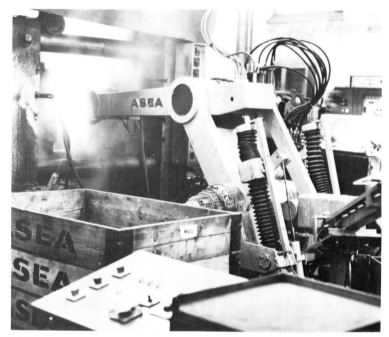

cleaner might see, say, a pocket calculator in the waste bin, fish it out, check to make sure it still works, and put it carefully back on the desk. The robot would scoop it up without a second thought, and woe betide its owner on Monday morning!

On the other hand, no-one has the mental energy to do a job that has no drudgery in it at all. When computer-aided design was first introduced to the aircraft industry a few years ago, the first – unlooked for – result was a strike among draftsmen at a British design consultancy who were using the equipment to design a new wing for some American military transport aircraft. Their complaint was just this: in the past they would be set a problem – design the outer aileron, say. They would sit down, have a think, wander round the office, chat to their friends, doodle upside down on the corners of their drawing boards, do a few sums in the train, have another think, and in three months feel their way to a good design out of all the millions of no-good possibilities. The computer put a stop to this pleasant process. As soon as they sketched in a possible solution, it would straighten up all the lines, dash in rows of rivets, go off to the master database, look up the loads this bit was supposed to bear and how heavy it could be, do the stress analysis in a few milliseconds and come back with the terse decision, 'No good. Try again.' The miserable designer's brain wasn't proposing to produce another drop of nectar for three months – the last one was only five hours ago! So the designers went on strike. They couldn't stand not having the spells of drudgery – what might be considered 'reflection time' in between bouts of creativity.

Fitting the computer in

Offices and factories are complex organisms, with many different processes and procedures. Perhaps the computer could, in theory, take over the whole operation; it is a very different matter to get the computer to take over a small part of the operation and to fit its procedures in with the procedures of the human beings it has to work with.

The present generation of office computers do not blend well with traditional paper procedures. Data has to be copied from invoices and typed into the electronic stock control and accounting programs; it has to be copied back again into letters of apology to creditors, and letters of menace to debtors.

To make ultimate sense of the technology, letters and documents of all sorts that come into a firm ought to be held on electronic file, in a form the computer can make immediate use

The 'paper-driven' office is friendly, comprehendable and in some ways inefficient. But most of this information is on scraps of paper which come from a large number of different sources. Could it ever be held in a computer's data bank? Is the paperless office (see here – below – at Citibank New York) really going to take its place overnight? Information here is stored and retrieved electronically, but it is only certain kinds of information that can easily be transmitted in this way – mainly that generated within the organisation and within the system. Unless all offices have compatible systems, the piece of paper, read by the human eye, will still keep its importance because of its flexibility.

of. At present they can't be, unless they are copy typed onto the machine, which is ridiculous. There is equipment which is able to read text into the computer, but it isn't yet available at under £50,000.

When a customer writes and says 'Please send me three dozen of your "Honolulu" style shorts and your Winter Catalogue when it's ready' the system ought automatically to raise a delivery note, an invoice, adjust the books – and, in six months time, send off a catalogue. Sadly, most software falls short of this and a clerk is still needed to finish off what the computer can't manage.

In factories there are similar limitations. In those designed to make things by traditional methods the advent of the computer has produced only little change – a computer-controlled machine here and there – maybe the occasional robot doing a nasty job, but no systematic exploitation of the possibilities. Yet in some places in the world – especially Japan – there are automatic factories (there was one in Britain until the recession forced it to close down). Goods come in, are handled, machined and assembled by flexible machines, each controlled by its local computer and linked to its fellow machines and to a central computer. Often the products have been re-designed in such a way that the new technology can handle them more easily.

In such factories the incoming orders, the checking of the progress of the manufacture of each item, the warehousing and the dispatch of the goods and of the attendant paperwork is integrated by a network of computers. Such factories are able to respond to the need for new products because the equipment is 'under software control'. A new product, designed with computer-aided design equipment linked directly with the computer-aided manufacturing process, can be 'fitted in' with ease. The use of such techniques by some forward-looking companies gives them many advantages over their competitors: they can respond to orders more quickly; products which don't sell can be removed and replaced without having to abandon 'dedicated' production lines; quality is on the whole higher and the labour content is lower, making the product cheaper.

The brewing industry is one of the best existing examples of automation in Britain, largely because breweries were being re-designed and rebuilt to mass-produce beer about 10 years ago. They are therefore laid out for automation. In a brewery, large tanks of liquids are mixed, heated, refrigerated and generally pumped about to produce the foaming delights of the saloon bar. Essentially, the machines only have to sense the levels and temperatures of liquid in various tanks. They have to open valves,

Flexible manufacturing
Below left: Computer-aided design of the parts required to press out vehicle body panels.

Below right: A computer-controlled template cutting machine.

Bottom: Robots working co-operatively, welding a truck. Automated production undoubtedly leads to increased productivity but it also requires new skills, with the loss of many traditional semi-skilled craft jobs.

and turn pumps on and off. The problems are basically simple. So, in some breweries, all the master brewer has to do is to go into work, and type on the keyboard of his microcomputer:

MAKE 10000 GALLONS OF OLD CATASTROPHE

In less well organised industries, the small computer has made much less headway.

The point is that unless the whole thing is thought through, the use of computers in industry – as in the office – is bound to be piecemeal and messy. We are, with the exception of those few (largely foreign) factories, or those very few completely electronic office systems, still in the early days of the new technology. And when it comes, there is a price to pay, of course – many skilled and semi-skilled craftsmen and clerks in these highly automated industries have lost their jobs. The jobs which remain are the highly skilled ones, those involving judgment or human contact (the designers, the technicians, the salesmen), the unskilled ones (the floor sweepers) and those doing jobs which are still too difficult or too expensive to mimic with a robot (crane drivers, for instance).

Linking computers together

We have already looked briefly (on page 28) at the way in which computers first stopped being isolated machines, locked away in their air-conditioned temples, being ministered to by the data processing high priests and launched out to join their users in the world outside.

Many of the timesharing systems which developed from early mainframe computing depended upon the use of several terminals linked to one central computer. A terminal is very much like the video display/keyboard unit that acts as an input/output medium for many microcomputers: it is a machine which provides input and output devices, and may contain a microprocessor to give it some 'intelligence', but which is dependent upon a larger processor for its computing power. The great advantage is that the terminal can be located wherever its user needs to be, while the main computer might be miles away from it. Many terminals today are portable, too.

What connects the terminal to the computer, then? It generally uses either the telephone system, or a private line which works in much the same way. The private line is more reliable in operation, but the telephone system is more flexible:

you can phone many computers from any convenient phone, link the terminal to the phone handset with a device called an acoustic coupler, and – if you know the machine's passwords – compute away.

The public computer

Not content with merely providing the lines through which computers and terminals can talk to each other, British Telecom has now gone one better and provided a computer which we can talk to. That's what Prestel is – a large central computer with a large amount of memory space, which British Telecom 'leases' out to private information providers. Any of us with a Prestel terminal, or a microcomputer with a Prestel adaptor, can dial the central computer and obtain the information stored on it.

Computers used as stores for information in this way are known as databanks, and this type of system, which uses the telephone network as a framework for providing databank information, is known as viewdata. A similar system, 'teletext', depends upon broadcast information, which is received on adapted television sets: Ceefax and Oracle are the British examples. These systems were developed in Britain and are being exploited all over the developed world.

Prestel, British Telecom's huge but as yet underused data bank. Is this the way we'll get more factual information in future or will we prefer traditional methods for shopping around?

Needless to say, the Prestel computer is just the same as all the other computers we have talked about, and it has to be programmed in the same sort of way to enable us to find our way around its stores of information. This is done using a kind of 'menu-driven' approach. (A menu-driven program is one which presents you with choices on the screen. Pushing the appropriate button then leads to further choices, progressively narrowing down the search until you find the information you're looking for.)

Microcomputers and viewdata

Microcomputers have the capability to retrieve and display information stored in these public databanks. Some have a teletext or viewdata card that plugs into one of the input/output ports. Microcomputers designed in Europe are now being designed from the start to be able to link with Prestel or teletext.

One problem in Britain is the need to get British Telecom approval before any device can be plugged into the telephone system and this limits the use of Prestel at the moment. However, some systems are designed around teletext modules, i.e. devices for receiving the broadcast information from the BBC or ITV and come in either kit or ready built form. To appreciate and use teletext or viewdata to the full, however, colour must be available, and this rules out many American or Japanese systems at the moment.

One of the more exciting developments is in the area of 'telesoftware', whereby the computer can receive programs via teletext or viewdata. The appropriate page can be dialled up, and then the program can be loaded directly into the computer.

Microcomputer networks

As well as using these databank facilities, many microcomputer users will be interested in communicating with other users: people with technical, business or hobby interests in common, for instance. The same kinds of system can be adapted to serve this purpose.

In America, private organisations are already offering data network facilities. Anybody with the appropriate equipment that allows the computer to link into the phone system – an acoustic coupler or a permanent connection of some kind – can join the network by enrolling once a year, and then pay a fee – around £1 an hour – to use the network. You can communicate with other microcomputer users, interrogate a central database, or even gain access to programs held centrally. Most of the popular computer systems are catered for. The quarterly telephone bill is usually the most expensive item!

Cutting out the cost of phone calls means investing in private lines, a desirable alternative if you plan to communicate regularly with a small number of other local machines. There are now a number of these 'networks', one of the best known being the 'Cambridge Ring'. This was developed by Cambridge University, to allow all their computers scattered around the town to talk to one another. The reason for this was simple. One computer may have some information that another one would find useful. Instead of duplicating the programming, or even shipping data around on vulnerable disc or tape, it was easier to link them all together with a few wires. The Cambridge Ring was originally designed for minicomputers and mainframes, although microcomputers can now link in with it.

Recent developments have produced cheap 'ring' circuitry that costs around £50 per computer. Although it's only available on one or two microcomputers at the moment, it is designed to be flexible enough so that eventually many different makes can be interconnected. Up to 255 individual computers can be linked together, and even share the same expensive disc drives and

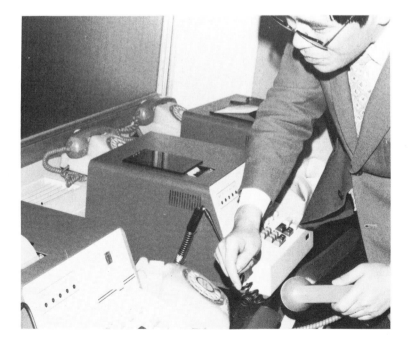

A Japanese 'network' of computer terminals for the small shopkeeper. A central computer takes in yesterday's electronically recorded sales details from each shop and automatically organises the deliveries of new stock and does the bookkeeping. But is it sapping initiative?

printers. This exciting development will probably lead to many groups of people in a locality or a building connecting their computers together and creating local networks. Schools are a prime example.

Computer networks in buiness The network idea is particularly useful in business, and on a large scale it is helping to provide the basis of a totally automated information handling system. How would it work?

The age of instant banking may be approaching. Computer networks within and between the banks could easily be expanded to reach the counter clerk and to the customer himself. Here the customer completes a transaction in under a minute by entering details on a simple keyboard, doing away with the need to write a cheque. The same system can even be extended into shops so that customers can pay their bills by debiting their bank accounts on the spot.

Take, for example, the office of a small magazine. It has the following staff: an editor, a production sub-editor, two reporters, an editorial secretary, an advertising manager, two salesmen and an advertising secretary. They could all have microcomputers on their desks, consisting of a screen, a keyboard and a processor and memory linked to a central hard disc and a high-speed printer. The editorial and advertising departments work mostly apart, but occasionally have to collaborate. Consider the editorial department first.

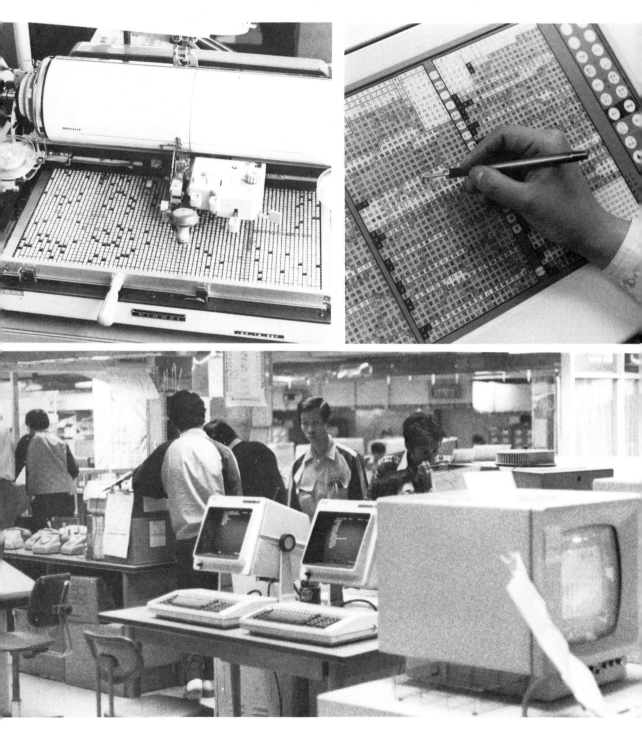

The editor and reporters write articles on their machines, which are stored on the hard disc. Articles are sent in by outside contributors, and are copy-typed, or read in by an optical character reader, one of those expensive devices which can transform text on paper into computer input, and also kept on the disc. When an issue is being made up, the editor puts a list of the articles he wants included on the disc, and the production editor uses that list to tell him what articles to pull into his computer for copy-editing. This involves checking spelling: he'll probably use a spelling correction program to help. It involves checking punctuation, and there will be a program to help with that too. When an article is satisfactory, he will put a header on it specifying what typeface it's to be set in, and send it down the telephone line to the printers.

Meanwhile, the editorial secretary has to pay the contributors. She has a program that looks at the finished articles, counts the number of words in each, looks up the contributor's file to see how much the editor has agreed to pay each writer, and calculates their fee. It can print out cheques ready for signature. It updates this file, so that later on it will be easy to see who wrote what, when and for how much.

Much of the editor's time is taken up in correspondence with readers and contributors, and he'll use his microcomputer to draft letters which his secretary will create – possibly incorporating standard phrases, or using complete standard letters in some cases – and get printed out. The letters will be filed electronically on the hard disc.

The advertising department will be able to use their computers to keep track of who has ordered what pages in what issue. They will note the agreed discounts, and at the end of the month a program will calculate what each advertiser owes and send out invoices. The computer will keep track of statistics on booking and revenues.

Sometimes an advertiser will ask to advertise in any issue which has an editorial feature mentioning his product. The advertising staff will search the articles on file to see if any include the name of his product and, if any do, to put a note in the file asking for notification when that article is going to be used.

Ideally, this office will have no paper in it at all. It will use quite a lot of expensive hardware, but the saving in time and efficiency will more than pay for it. The people in the office will use standard software packages for word processing and database management – controlling files on the disc – but they may even write a lot of programs themselves, too.

In some ways, a magazine is ideally suited to the computer age. Its staff do routine things to a mass of text. The final step might be to do away with the printed magazine completely, and that *could* happen, no doubt, in a few years. The material could be distributed by wire to people's homes, and displayed on their television screens, or printed out on their (by now) cheap printers and paid for in their telephone bills.

There are many other businesses that could go the same way. One effect will be to cut down the numbers of supporting staff. In principle – it will doubtless take some time to realise – such an organisation will not need an elaborate accounts department. It won't need lots of typists producing and filing invoices. The people who work there will deal directly with the creative parts of their jobs, leaving the computers to do the boring bits. That, in turn, will cut down the numbers of managers.

Several such units can be connected together via larger computers. A big company might, in five years' time, consist of a number of small, energetic profit centres which do their business on a local network, while feeding selected information into the firm's central minicomputer. The magazine, for instance, might be part of a larger group. Once a month, perhaps, the advertising department could run a program which totals the number of pages sold, the total amount of money taken and send it to a file for the attention of the managing director, where it's combined with similar results from other enterprises.

The Portable office.
All you need is a 'phone. Plug the handset into the rubber cups at the back of this portable terminal and you can contact the computer in your office from home or from a hotel room anywhere in the world. Stored text – memos or messages – can be transmitted and received automatically. Journalists on some American newspapers send in their copy in this way.

So, what would the visitor notice in such an office? Firstly, the keyboard and screen on every desk. Secondly, the relative tidyness of the desks; there would be very little paper lying about. Thirdly, the absence of filing cabinets; all the unit's files will be kept on the hard disc unit, which lives in a desk drawer. Fourthly, someone having a nervous breakdown in the corner because it's all too complicated. . . .

The most noticeable thing about the office might well be that it isn't where you might expect it to be. Once you handle information electronically, there is much less need for people to be physically close to each other. The magazine's staff might want to be together, because a lot of their work consists in sharing their experience with each other but there is no real need for them to be in the same building as their managers, or as the other magazines of the same group. Some of the staff of one magazine might prefer to work at home in Chiswick, others in Wiltshire.

Instead of mail, the staff would use the telephone network to send information to each other. Their contributors would be encouraged to write their articles on their machines at home, and to send them in by telephone – possibly by satellite, too, if they live abroad.

If humans want to work this way it is now, or will soon be, technically, quite possible. The limits to the speed of change will largely be due to human reactions to change. Will we *allow* ourselves to work in this way?

The cheap, home facsimile copier linked to the telephone (this one is French). Could it make electronic mail a real possibility? Is this how we might one day get our newspapers and letters?

Using Prestel in business

As well as linking their own computers together, business people can also use the Prestel computer and the other kinds of public network we've talked about.

As one example, the contributors to the imaginary magazine we described above might well send in their offerings through Prestel. They would connect their computers to the telephone line, dial up the Prestel number, 'access' the magazine's message page, and write onto it the article they want to submit. Later on, the magazine's computer would make a routine check of the message page, find something there and load it into its own files and put a note in the editor's message file.

There are also going to be wider opportunities for selling information through Prestel. For instance, you might be thinking of making a journey and have a program in your computer at home to check British Rail's timetables to work out a route with times of trains and fares (in other words, a variation on the 'route-finding' program we wrote in Chapter 4). Perhaps, as is more likely, you wouldn't want to write this program yourself, so you would 'rent' it for a day from some software supplier, paying a small fee which is automatically added to your telephone bill.

You might want to buy or sell something – let's say, a second-hand car. Businesses that today publish weekly lists of advertisements in newspapers could start to do the same thing on their computers. An advertiser would use his computer to put directly onto his disc what it is he has to sell. Just like an advertiser in 'Exchange and Mart', for instance, he'd have to learn certain conventions which people use. One route down his program 'menu' might run:

```
SECTION = CARS
TYPE = FORD
MODEL = CONSUL
LITRES = 2
YEAR = 1977
MILEAGE = 500
PRICE = 3000
TEL NO. 221 5000
```

He would probably be charged a fee for putting his advertisement up and a further daily rate until he took it out.

Enquirers would use their machines in much the same way. They'd send a message like this:

```
MAKE–FORD
LITRES⟨3
PRICE⟨2000
MILEAGE⟨10000
```

and get back every car that matches this description.

The great advantage of a networked system like this is that it is possible for buyers and sellers to contact each other directly – not only by receiving a phone number, for instance, but by leaving messages on the system itself. They could even pay for the goods through the computer, giving their credit card number!

Beyond seeing that it is all possible, it is hard for us now to foresee how this business will develop. The whims and preferences of users will be so important that they will dictate how growth happens. The system offers enormous flexibility, but it is up to its users to determine which of the possible paths of development are taken.

The future?

In future the speed of change may not be governed so much by the limits of technology as by our reaction to it. If humans want to live and work in the ways we have described it is now, or soon will be, technically quite possible. The automatic factory already exists in Japan. The highly automated magazine publishing house already exists, in effect, in America.

But it is sobering to remember that the experimental British automatic factory mentioned above was closed down recently because it seemed a low priority compared with other activities in the recession. It is also sobering to look at the history of attempts to introduce new technology – much of it computerised – in the printing and publishing industries in Britain.

However, it is quite possible to look forward to a time when all these amazing labour-saving worlds co-exist. And jobs? What will most people then do when the craftsmen, the clerks, the middle managers become unnecessary? Will we create a society in which to work is not seen as an essential part of life, essential to one's self-respect? or will we create new jobs in the 'caring' industries – health, education, welfare? Will new kinds of personal services – hitherto undreamed of – be created in a luxurious Brave New World? Will the working day and the working week become shorter? Or will we create a divided society where some have work and some do not?

Window on the world and window on the home.

An experimental two-way computer-managed community television system. This Japanese lady can call up a range of services on her television set and take part in community television programmes and adult education classes using her own television camera and microphone. The keypad helps her to select channels, and videotext-type information, and makes it possible for her to vote on local issues at the press of a button.

It is possible – and indeed fascinating – to speculate about what the future may bring. We really can't know – although one thing is certain: there will be change and there will be challenge. Choices will have to be made and decisions are best made against a background of knowledge. If this technology *is* capable of changing our lives then it is best that we understand it so that we can help it along if it seems good, and challenge it if it seems bad. We hope that this book – and the whole BBC Computer Literacy Project – has helped to provide a little of that understanding.

Future Past – future perfect? This romanticised view of the future appeared
in the 1969 catalogue of Nieman-Marcus the up-market American
superstore. For $10,000 the woman who has everything could buy a
computer for her kitchen to help with household accounts and 'to find that
little recipe'. Today the store doesn't sell computers because 'everyone has
one'. Since 1969 there has been a revolution in hardware and hundreds of
thousands of microcomputers have been sold. Yet a similar revolution in
software is still to come.

Glossary

Up till now the world of computers has been dominated by specialists who revel in using jargon. Whereas much jargon is unnecessary and makes communication difficult between those in the know and those outside, there are many technical terms which are useful and important; some, indeed, are coming into common use as the effects of computers spread. This glossary should help to explain the most widely used terms.

Accumulator A place in the computer where one number can temporarily be brought (for example from a part of the memory) and where, amongst other things, another number can be added to it, subtracted from it or compared with it.

Acoustic coupler A gadget which enables audible tones, say from a telephone, to be turned into the digital form which the computer can understand (and vice-versa).

Address In the computer, information in the form of numbers is moved around from place to place. Each place has an 'address' which is itself a number. In a way it is like the number of a house in a street.

ALGOL One of a number of high level languages (q.v.) – often used by mathematicians.

Algorithm Although we have avoided the use of this word in the book, it means the solution to a problem – say, on paper – which could then lead to the series of instructions which make up a computer program. However, the term does not necessarily have anything to do with computing.

Alphanumeric A mixture of characters which can be numbers or letters or symbols like '@' or any combination. The typewriter or computer keyboard is an 'alphanumeric' keyboard.

Analogue A quantity (like temperature or time) which is continuously varying – as opposed to digital (q.v.). Most things in the natural world are analogue. When we measure them and give them a numerical value, we digitise them.

A/D converter – Analogue to digital converter	(See under CONVERTER.)
Applications program (or applications software)	A computer program designed for a particular outside purpose – it might be for a business application or a game or be an educational program. As opposed to systems software (see Software).
Arithmetic & logic unit (ALU)	An area in the central processor of the computer where arithmetical and logical processes (such as comparing two numbers) take place.
Array	In effect an orderly list or a table of numbers or words (data) where every position is labelled and can be handled separately or in a sequence by the computer.
Artificial intelligence	The ability of a computer (or computer-controlled machine) to perform a task which, if a human being were to perform the same task, would be said to require 'intelligence'. This begs the question, of course of what is meant by 'intelligence'. Often the computer will learn from experience and improve its performance of a particular task.
ASCII	'American Standard Code for Information Interchange'. The internationally accepted code which represents numbers, letters and symbols with unique binary code values which the computer can then deal with.
Assembly language ('assembler')	A low level language which uses mnemonics rather than ordinary words to give instructions to the computer. These mnemonics translate directly into the binary instructions which the computer understands in a much more economical way than does a high level language in that they take up less memory space. But it is less approachable for beginners.
Author language	A 'very high level' language program which enables those not skilled in programming in, say, BASIC, to write applications programs easily because the author language (itself written in, say, BASIC) requires little more than the writing of instructions in ordinary English.
Backing storage	Any outside storage medium (usually magnetic tape or disc) which supports and can be linked to the main memory in the computer. When the power is off, information in the backing storage is not lost. The capacity of a backing storage memory is much greater than the computer's internal working memory.

Bar code A pattern of printed lines on an object identifying it and containing information about it which can be read into the computer by scanning it with a light pen. Common now on grocery packaging.

BASIC The most popular 'high level language' for microcomputers. Stands for 'Beginners All-purpose Symbolic Instruction Code'. Chapter 4 is devoted to it.

Baud rate This is a measure of the number of bits per second travelling from one part of a computer system (e.g. a cassette filing system) to another, or between computers.

Binary A way of counting using only two alternative values – 0 or 1, 'on' or 'off', 'black' or 'white'. Deep inside, computers like binary – indeed they can understand nothing else.

Bit A binary digit – a '0' or a '1' (see binary).

Branch A part of a computer program where a choice is made between alternative routes – the 'intelligence factor' in computing.

Bug A defect or mistake in a computer program.

Bus A set of electrical pathways or connectors inside a computer.

Byte 'By eight'. Usually means a group of eight bits. One byte contains enough information to represent one ASCII character.

CAD Stands for 'computer aided design'.

CAL Stands for 'computer aided learning'.

Cassette tape The 'cheap & cheerful' way of storing programs and data for a microcomputer, using a domestic tape recorder (see backing storage).

CEEFAX The BBC's broadcast screen information service. Part of the television signal is used to send data which can then be displayed on the screen of a suitable television set. A form of viewdata (q.v.).

Central processing unit The control 'brain' of the computer where all parts of the computer system are linked together and where the calculations and manipulation of data take place.

Characters	The all-purpose expression for numerals, letters & symbols which a computer can print or display on a screen.
Chip	A single device containing many transistors and other components formed on the surface of a piece of silicon. When packaged up, looks like a centipede because of its many metal legs.
COBOL	A high level language usually used for business applications.
Command	A direct instruction to the computer which it carries out at once.
Compatible	Two computers are said to be compatible if a program written on one will run on the other without modification.
Compiler	A program inside the computer which converts a complete program – like an applications program – written in a high level language into the machine code version which the computer needs to be able to run it.
Computer and computing	The whole of this book is about the meaning of these two words. In a nutshell the computer is a device which can process information according to instructions given to it by human beings and in this way perform useful or entertaining tasks. Computing is the art or science of getting the computer to do what you want.
Converter analogue to digital (or vice-versa)	A device for converting analogue information (coming from the real world) in the form of a continuously varying electrical voltage from some kind of electrical sensor into the digital form which the computer can cope with – or the reverse.
Crash	A computer is said to 'crash' when a program which is running cannot be completed and cannot be restarted.
Cursor	Some way of marking the screen with the position at which the next character typed in at the keyboard will appear.
Daisy wheel printer	A printer which makes use of a plastic disc around the edge of which is a set of print characters. The wheel rotates at speed until the required character is brought before a hammer which strikes it against a ribbon. One wheel can easily be replaced with another with a different typeface.
Data	Loosely, means 'information' which a computer program can deal with. Data can be in the form of numbers or characters.

Database	A self-important sounding word meaning an organised collection of files of information to which the computer has access. If many people have access to it through different terminals it might then qualify to be called a data bank.
De-bugging	The business of testing a program and then changing it to get rid of 'bugs' or faults.
Dialect	A version of a particular computer language e.g. PET BASIC, BBC BASIC, RML BASIC – all are different dialects of BASIC with some things in common, others not.
Digital	To do with numbers, c.f. 'Analogue'.
Disc or 'floppy' disc	A flat magnetic disc on which programs and data may be stored and retrieved quickly – far faster than cassette tape but more expensive (sometimes 'disk').
Dot matrix printer	A printer using a series of electrically 'hammered' moving pins to create characters composed of a pattern of dots.
EPROM	Stands for erasable, programmable read-only memory – a chip which can be fed with a program and which will hold it until it is erased (usually by exposing the surface of the chip to ultraviolet light). After that it can be re-programmed. (See PROM, ROM).
Expert system	(See Artificial Intelligence.) Crudely, expert systems are able to make decisions in areas normally dependent on professional judgement – e.g. medicine, law, oil prospecting.
File	An organised collection of information – e.g. computer programs.
Firmware	A program permanently held in a 'read only memory' chip in a computer. The term usually refers to the programs which manage the internal operations of the computer rather than applications programs, though these, too, could be 'blown' into firmware.
Floppy disc	(See disc.)
Flow chart	A diagram on paper showing the sequence of events and choices which need to be made in the solution of a problem – usually (though not exclusively) relating to a computer program.
FORTRAN	A high level language mainly for scientific and mathematical use.

Garbage	Meaningless or unwanted data coming from the computer and arising from a number of causes. This has given rise to the maxim 'Garbage in, garbage out' and the acronym 'GIGO'.
Graphics	The overall term meaning the appearance of pictures or diagrams on the screen as opposed to letters and numbers.
Handshaking	A 'dialogue' between two computers or a computer and a 'peripheral device' – like a printer – which establishes that a message is passed between them to their mutual satisfaction.
Hardware	The physical bits and pieces of the computer – as opposed to the 'software' or the programs.
Hard copy	Tangible and permanent output from a computer, on paper.
Hexadecimal or 'HEX'	An arcane way of counting based not on base 2 (binary) or on base 10 (decimal) but on base 16. Understood by people who program in low level languages. One 'byte' (q.v.) can be represented by two hexadecimal symbols, hence its significance.
High level language	A programming language where the programmer uses instructions which are close to his ordinary familiar language rather than machine code. In effect, the higher the 'level' of the language the nearer it is to ordinary language and the easier it is for the uninitiated to understand.
Integrated circuit (IC)	The circuits combined together on the surface of a silicon chip. IC is often synonymous with 'chip'.
Interactive	A way of operating where the user is in direct and continual two way communication with the computer, maybe answering its questions and receiving its reactions to the answers.
Input	The route whereby information gets into the computer or the putting in of information by the operator (say from a keyboard).
Instruction	A computer program consists of a series of instructions, often used interchangably (though perhaps wrongly) with 'commands'.
Interface	The boundary between two parts of a computer system. Often the boundary consists of a piece of electronic circuitry. Even more inelegant, as a verb, meaning to make one part of a computer system run smoothly with another.

Interpreter	A program living inside the computer which translates the keywords in a high level language program, line by line, as it runs into a more compact form which the processor can cope with.
Keyboard	One form of input device for a computer. Keyboards are usually 'Alphanumeric' (q.v.) but also contain special keys which perform particular functions on the computer.
Keywords	Words in the vocabulary of a high level language which have a special meaning to the computer.
Kilo	A prefix meaning a thousand – e.g. kilobyte – a thousand 'bytes'. A prefix meaning approximately a thousand (actually it is 2 to the power of 10, which is 1024).
Language	A computer 'language' can hardly be considered as the same as, say, a language like French or German but it is an organised way of communicating with a computer using precisely defined instructions.
LCD	Liquid crystal display. Most pocket calculators and digital watches have these. The characters usually appear as black against a light background. The effect is a chemical one, which uses up very little electrical power.
LED	Light emitting diode. An electronic component which emits light when excited by an electric current.
Location	A place in the computer's memory where information is to be stored (see address).
Low level language	(See machine code.)
Machine code	The pattern of '0s' and '1s' which the computer actually understands. It is the lowest level of language for a programmer to work in and all high level programs are concerted into machine code instructions automatically when they run (though not in the most efficient way, hence the need for programming directly in a low level language, since programs written directly in a low level language run faster than those in high level language.)
Memory	A computer's memory is a device or series of devices capable of storing information temporarily or permanently in the form of patterns of binary '1s' and '0s'. The computer then 'reads'

information from the memory or in some cases also 'writes' information into it when it operates.

1 Internal Memory – this usually consists of silicon chips within the body of the computer. Some of these memory chips will contain information which is permanently held there and which can only be 'read' and is not erased when the computer is switched off ('non-volatile', 'read-only memory'). Other chips represent the working memory of the computer where information can be stored temporarily when a program is running and which is lost when the computer is switched off ('volatile', 'random access memory'). The computer's capacity at any one time for handling information is limited. Consequently there is a need to have a 'back-up' memory outside the computer.

2 External Memory. This usually consists of a magnetic tape or disc on which binary information is stored and 'called up' by the computer as required. The information is not lost when the computer is switched off.

Menu-driven programs	Programs which present the operator with a list of choices at any particular time and these are displayed on the screen for him to choose from. Each choice leads down a different branch of the program.
Micro	Has two meanings – (i) 'small' – as in 'microcomputer' – and (ii) a millionth of something – e.g. microsecond, a millionth of a second.
Microcomputer	A small computer system built round a microprocessor but having all the necessary bits and pieces (peripherals and memory) to link with the outside world and store information.
Microelectronics	The use of electrical devices in which many different components are formed together (integrated) into microscopically small circuits on the surface of single 'chips' (usually of silicon).
Microprocessor	Sometimes used as a synonym for microcomputer but, more correctly, a microprocessor is the central chip containing the control unit for the computer.
Minicomputer	A medium sized computer of the kind which might be used by a medium sized company to keep its records, work out its payroll, stock control, etc. Midway between a 'micro' and a 'mainframe' computer.

Network	A system where a number of computers, terminals and other components (like printers and disc drives) can be linked together electronically – sometimes over some distance.
Numeric	To do with numbers.
Operating systems	The software program sitting permanently inside the computer which supervises the running of applications programs and controls the operations of the various input and output devices like the video display unit, keyboard, etc.
Output	Information which a computer sends out to a screen or a printer or to a backing memory store.
Paddle	Another name for a joystick control – e.g. for a T.V. game.
Parallel	When electrical patterns of bits travel simultaneously along parallel wires they are said to be a 'parallel' bit stream.
Pascal	A high level language preferred by many to BASIC for general programming work.
Package	A word used to describe a computer program or collection of programs written to be useful to a number of people (as opposed to one written and tailored for a specific purpose for one client).
PCB (printed circuit board)	The plastic board into which the computer's various electronic components are soldered. These are linked by thin interconnecting wires printed on its surfaces.
Peripherals	Bits and pieces of a computer system which connect in different ways with the central processor and memory and which form its input and output devices. Peripherals include printers, disc drives, joy sticks, graphics tablets, light pens, etc.
Port	A place where electrical connection can be made with the central processor in the computer.
Portability	Programs are portable if they run on different computer systems.
Prestel	The name given by British Telecom to the first public viewdata service (q.v.) using the public telephone system.
Processor	(See central processing unit.)

Program	A series of instructions which the computer carries out in sequence. As a verb, to write these instructions.
PROM (Programmable Read Only Memory)	A chip which can be programmed by the user. Once programmed, its contents are 'non-volatile'. (See also ROM, EPROM.)
RAM (Random Access Memory)	Memory into which information can be put (written) and from which it can instantly be copied (read) no matter where it is in the memory. RAM is the 'working memory' of the computer into which applications programs can be loaded from outside and then run. Sometimes called a read/write memory.
Real time	A computer system is said to be operating in 'real time' if the processing of information fed in takes place virtually at once.
ROM (Read Only Memory)	A memory circuit in which the information stored in 'built into' the chip when it is made and which cannot subsequently be changed by the user. Information can be copied from ROM but it cannot be written there – hence the name read only memory. Another name for read only memory is 'firmware' since this implies software which is permanent or firmly in place, on a chip.
Robot	A computer-controlled device which is fitted with sensors and activating mechanisms. The sensors receive information about the surrounding environment, send it to a computer which then decides on the basis of its program how the mechanical parts should respond – e.g. to pick something up or to move about. Some robots can be programmed to improve their performance as a result of their experience, (see artificial intelligence).
Scanning	This word usually refers to the very rapid examination of every item in a computer's 'list' of data to see if some condition is met.
Serial	When electrical patterns of bits travel one after the other down a wire in a computer they are said to be a 'serial' bit stream – as opposed to a 'parallel' bit stream (q.v.).
Silicon	The chemical element which is used as the basis for the increasingly more complex integrated electronic circuits which recently have been responsible for the 'microelectronics revolution'. Silicon is present in sand (which is silicon dioxide). It has odd electrical properties, sometimes conducting electricity and sometimes not, depending, for example, on what other substances are mixed with it in minute quantities.

Software The general term which refers to all computer programs which can be run on computer hardware. A distinction can be made between the programs responsible for the running of the computer – its internal 'housekeeping' and operating systems and so on – and 'applications programs', (q.v.). Ultimately, all software consists of patterns of binary information which give the computer its marching orders.

Statement Another name for an instruction used as part of a computer program.

Storage Another word for memory – a place where information can be kept in a form which is accessible to the computer.

String A set of characters one after the other which the computer can deal with. The last sentence could be thought of as a string – note that spaces count as 'characters'. A distinction is usually made between strings and numbers. The computer can perform arithmetic on numbers but not on characters. Thus 4711 could be a 'string' – simply four characters which could, for example, be written backwards as 1174. Alternatively it could be a number – four thousand seven hundred and eleven – which can be multiplied or divided (etc.). However it would be meaningless to say that the 'number' 4711 could be written backwards.

Systems analyst A person trained in the analysis of complex physical or organisational problems and able to offer solutions calling on a range of skills, one of which may involve the use of the computer and computer programming.

Tape Magnetic tape or punched paper tape can both be used to store computer programs or data. Neither is as fast as disc systems when it comes to finding the information stored but they do have advantages – cheapness, for example.

Telesoftware Computer programs sent by telephone line or by television as part of the teletext signal. With a suitable decoder the computer program can be entered directly into the memory of a computer and then 'run'. A new development.

Teletext An information service sent as a small part of the broadcast television signal. With a suitable decoder the information can be displayed on the home television screen as a series of 'pages'. The BBC's service is called CEEFAX; the IBA's is ORACLE.

Terminal	A peripheral device usually consisting of a keyboard and a screen which can link into a computer network sometimes using a telephone line as the link.
Time-sharing	A way of sharing out powerful computer facilities between a number of users who want those facilities at the same time on a number of separate terminals. Each user gets the impression that he has sole use of the computer.
Transistor	An electronic device which can act as a switch or an amplifier. Individual transistors are found in portable radio sets and amplifiers, but the transistor is also the building block of the integrated circuit on the silicon chip, one of which may contain thousands of transistors.
Variable	An electronic 'box' or pigeon hole into which data can be put and subsequently be changed. A variable has a name and a value. The name does not change but the value can. Variables can also be 'numeric' or 'string' variables.
VDU (Visual Display Unit)	A television-like screen on which the output of the computer can be displayed. The VDU is the most usual 'output peripheral device' of the computer.
Videotex	(Synonymous with viewdata.)
Viewdata	A way of receiving digital information at a distance and displaying it on a television-like screen. Viewdata can involve telephone lines or television signals. (See Teletext, Prestel.)
Voice recognition	The ability of a computer to match the pattern of signals coming into it from a microphone with stored 'templates' held in its electronic memory and thus recognise words.
Voice synthesis	The ability of the computer to use stored patterns of sounds within its memory to assemble words which can be played through a loudspeaker.
Volatile memory	Memory in which information is lost when the power is switched off.
Wand	A pen-like device able to read optically coded labels (see bar codes).

Winchester disc	A powerful form of back-up storage for a computer. It consists of a rigid magnetic disc in a sealed container scanned by a head which does not quite touch the disc, therefore not wearing it out.
Word	When a computer operates it deals with groups of bits at a time. The minimum number of bits which the central processor handles at any one moment is called a 'word'. In a microcomputer the word is usually eight bits long.
Wordprocessing	A powerful new office procedure for electronically storing, editing and manipulating text using an electronic keyboard, computer and printer. The text is recorded on a magnetic medium rather than on paper, except for the final 'print-out'.

Index

Italic figures refer to captions to illustrations, 'gl.' means an entry in the glossary.